THE
Heartist
JOURNEY

*A Sacred Return
to the Woman Within*

STACIE SHOLER

ISBN: 979-8-9998139-1-6
E-Book ISBN: 979-8-9998139-0-9

www.staciemarie.love

For every soul who finds themselves here,
whether by chance or divine design—
this is for you.
For the seekers who have felt the ache of longing,
the wanderers who have walked through shadows in search of light,
and the tender-hearted who dare to return home to themselves.
May these pages be a mirror,
reflecting the beauty, strength, and truth already alive within you.
May they remind you that the love you seek
has been patiently waiting—
in the quiet chambers of your own heart—
all along.
This is your journey, too.
Welcome home.

CONTENTS

Introduction 1

Chapter 1: Listen to Your Intuition 19

Chapter 2: Feng Shui 46

Chapter 3: My Companion, William 62

Chapter 4: The Summer of 2013 75

Chapter 5: Open Your Heart 88

Chapter 6: Healing Codependency 99

Chapter 7: The Broken Road 113

Chapter 8: When the Soul Knows 133

Epilogue 149

About the Author 153

Dear Reader:

This book found you at the perfect time to support you on your spiritual and creative path. I'm your guide, Stacie Sholer.

As a Reiki master, shaman, artist, entura art therapist, and spiritual mentor who has spent decades studying emotional intelligence, the field of human potential & spirituality, I guide people to create love and harmony in their lives through unique creative tools.

In this book, you'll learn about my awakening journey, the individuals who supported me on that quest, and the tools I've used. You will also learn how to deepen your connection to yourself in a method I created called "The Heartist Journey."

These chapters examine everything from healing old trauma to relationships, pets, finances, and careers.

As an artist, I leaned into as many modalities as possible to guide me on my pilgrimage as I learned how to create harmony between my mind and heart. I came to understand how to create from the foundation of my heart and not my mind. My foundation is now built from my soul.

Today, I foster a nurturing space and a compassionate community where comfort, healing, and spiritual growth intertwine.

You could feel overwhelmed, anxious, unfulfilled, or searching for something, but you don't know what will quench your thirst. This book will help you get out of your busy mind and drop into your heart by exploring your creativity through art and other creative outlets.

As you read further into these pages, you will learn how to connect or reconnect with yourself and create more space in your home and life. You'll also be offered insight into healing from the past and cultivating a deeper sense of self-awareness and peace. In addition, we'll move through methods that will give you insight into your next heart's desires and dreams.

By connecting with yourself and deepening the love within, you can navigate life's journey authentically and operate harmoniously with the world around you — ultimately discovering the best path for your soul.

You'll find quick tips related to the chapter material at the end of every chapter. You'll also find questions to ponder or discuss within your book club. Finally, you'll find spaces to capture your thoughts about each section and fun mandalas to use as coloring breaks.

I'm so glad you found The Heartist Journey. I pray this book supports you as much as it did me. Ultimately, I hope this book helps you find peace within and come home to yourself.

As always, I bless all of this, or something better be done. Because why wouldn't you want to have something better than your wildest dreams?

And so it is.

Amen.

INTRODUCTION

M Y SPIRITUAL JOURNEY STARTED IN IDAHO.

At 21 years old, my son invited me to Sandpoint, Idaho, to witness his rite of passage from his year-long personal development program. I stood in awe as he proclaimed his vision for his life. Meanwhile, deep inside, I craved my vision and direction. And that's when a healer named Kristy and a trip to Italy fell into my lap.

After witnessing my son's growth, I gave myself the gift of a weekend of life coaching!

Kristy coached me in a way I had never experienced before. Through her leadership, she taught me ways to heal through hikes, feeling the heartbeat of a tree, sandpaintings, and even ceremonies with flowers and water.

It was strange at first. After all, I had healing sessions with stones and rattles that weekend. We had picnics and played at the park in the name of life coaching.

And my first homework assignment from Kristy was to get dressed up and take myself out on a date.

So, I dressed up in a new outfit, went to a really nice restaurant on the lake, and afterwards, walked out on the deck to the lake and had someone take a picture of me. There were lights all around the deck, and I felt like a movie star.

Being in nature at that time was very foreign to me. I remember the day Kristy asked me to feel a tree. To feel its heartbeat and truly connect to it. I couldn't feel anything at that time.

But the more I did it, the better I got at it. Within some time, I could recognize the need to release all the pent-up fear, anger, and resentment I had stored up.

My coaching experiences prior to Kristy were always indoors, and we always talked about things that happened in my life. I felt like a broken record.

Before working with Kristy, coaching and therapy had been about the same old stories I relived over and over again. I never fully healed with that type of coaching or therapy. It was more like placing a bandage on a wound.

After a week with Kristy, I wanted more. I asked her how she learned her way of healing, and she said some of it was through her training to become a shaman. I didn't know what that meant then, though I knew how I felt. I wanted more. I wanted to learn how to heal myself at a deeper level and help others do the same. I told her I wanted to go through the training, and she connected me with the same woman, the same shaman who trained her.

I spoke with her on the phone and started with her in the next session, which was about two months later.

Within months of experiencing my first healing by way of water, fire and rattle, I found myself right smack dab in the middle of a training called the Medicine Wheel.

The Medicine Wheel was a year of training in Sandpoint, Idaho. Although I lived in Arizona, I would fly there every three months to immerse myself in deep and vigorous personal development and spiritual training.

When my training in Idaho was finished, I craved more. After a few months of living my day-to-day life, I enrolled in a workshop with a teacher named Alison Armstrong. I signed up for her first class, and at that class, I committed to taking everything else she offered. At the beginning of her training, it was fun. I loved her books, and then came the workshops. The workshops were very spiritual and went very deep.

With Alison, I learned about men and the different phases of development they go through in life, about myself, and what I needed to be happy. I also learned about partnerships versus relationships.

I learned how I used to seek happiness outside of myself, in relationships, work, money, sex, food, and everything else I sought out. Through her work, I shifted the way I saw and related to men. I also shifted how I saw and treated myself, which equated to my relationships shifting more deeply, connected, and compassionately.

A few months after completing Alison's training, I was called to go on a solo journey to Europe. I had never traveled to Europe, though I had always wanted to go. I immediately signed up. I thought, "I can do this." I was ready to go. What I didn't know at that time, what I wasn't prepared for, was the internal battle I would have with myself to go on this trip from the moment I signed up until I actually was seated on that airplane. I didn't realize how difficult it was for me then to do something for myself that would grow me into becoming the woman I was meant to be.

For years after saying yes to this opportunity, I backed out. I just couldn't get myself to get on the plane. Fear had a hold of me.

The paperwork was filled out, I had bags, and I even had time off work. I just didn't have the courage to actually do it. I was going through so many feelings.

How could I take a month off from work?

This isn't financially responsible.

What if something came up with my kids, my family, my employee, and so much more?

I was so busy taking care of everyone else for most of my life I had forgotten how to take care of myself. I had nothing left inside of me, I was emotionally exhausted, I had forgotten what it was like to laugh, to feel deep love, to just be present in a conversation. I was attached to my email and worked like it was in my bloodstream.

If I stopped or took some time off what would I do with myself?

Finally, after three years of fear, I took the most significant leap of faith I could.

Not only did I finally say YES to a European trip alone, but I also retired from a company I had built for 20 years.

Now I had to go. There weren't any excuses left for me to use.

That day, I finally said yes to Italy, and it was etched into my brain.

Before I paid my trip to Italy in full, Kristy shared that the leaders of this group would be taking another group of women to Ireland a week or so after Italy. After doing a few more rounds of deliberating with myself, I added Ireland onto my trip!

Once I overcame my limiting beliefs, my fears, my internal battles, I paid what was left of my trip balance to Alchemy Adventures. Next I called the travel agent that was referred to me by Kristy.

I remember feeling overwhelmed. I was traveling to another country for the first time in my life and alone. I had never envisioned going to Italy and Ireland for the first time alone. I always pictured this type of trip being with the man I love, the love of my life, but instead, I was living it much differently than I dreamed about for most of my life. So, I swallowed my pride and followed my bliss, aka my heart, instead.

4

As I purchased my airline ticket to Italy, a country I had never been to, butterflies filled my belly. My throat clenched and dried up. Beads of sweat formed on my palms, and my heart kicked up a beat or two.

The travel agent was an angel; she helped me work through my feelings and supported me every step of the way. She shared an app with me where I could look at what I wanted to do while there; that was so much fun. I was already starting to practice living in the moment before I even left. I loved being in a position where I could pick everything I had always wanted to do. It felt so freeing to be open to choosing things for myself without having to ask permission from anyone or feeling obligated to ask if it were something they would want to do. When just months before, I had no idea what that meant, what I would like to do, what made my heart sing.

As I began to peruse the app, I began to know what made my heart sing. I picked painting classes, cooking classes, and wine tasting, even though I wasn't a wine person.

I picked castle touring, hot air balloon rides, horseback riding, the opera, a gondola ride, and so much more. I wanted to see Cinque Terre because I loved the pictures I saw on the internet when I searched for places in Italy, so I added that to the places I would go while there, too. Cinque Terre was so vivid and colorful; the houses were all different colors, the streets were all cobblestones, and so were all the places I traveled to in Italy. The houses were all stacked next to and on top of each other, nestled on what appeared to be mountains overlooking the sea. I found places I wanted to cook in Tuscany and tour the wineries. I wanted to go and see where Romeo and Juliette lived, the Colosseum, I went on a water taxi in Venice, traveled by train from Florence to Venice, and so much more. I was finally getting excited to go on my trip, and so I packed and headed to the airport for a life-changing journey where I would not return the same woman as when I left.

I was headed away to spend time in Italy solo for about a week before I met up with the ladies and one captain from Alchemy Adventures. I was feeling so many emotions, my adrenaline of excitement was the emotion that overrode it all! I flew into Rome first and had to switch planes in an airport where almost everyone spoke Italian. I took a week of Duolingo training on an app to learn Italian before I came here! Thankfully, most of the people I encountered spoke both English and Italian. I switched planes successfully and headed to the airport in Florence. I was so nervous when I got off the plane, praying I would be able to figure out where my luggage was and get to my first hotel, otherwise known as the "safety zone."

The taxi dropped me off right in front, and I checked into my hotel, where I would stay for a week before meeting the ladies for the backpacking trip at the train station. I went to my hotel room and remembered it being so small and cute. I knew I would only be there to sleep, so I wasn't very concerned about the aesthetics. I was, however, bummed that there wasn't a bathtub, which is what I took every day at home, time to create a "new normal". One of the things I thought was weird and both genius was how the lights would only stay on if you had the room key placed into it. At first, this was challenging to get used to, and then I just flowed with it.

Once in my room, I got situated and ended up staying up for a few hours even though it was very late back home when I arrived. I decided I would stay up until late so I could shake off this jet lag as quickly as possible. I went to eat at the restaurant just outside of the hotel, as mine only provided breakfast. Eating in Italy was very different from eating in the States.

Everything was fresh, the portions were huge, and the servers would not disturb you while you were eating. I had to ask for the check every time I ate out because in Italy, meals were to connect with each other and squeeze as much time as you wanted out of it. Eating was an event, an experience, something I learned I took for granted in the U.S. At home, I would eat as fast as possible so I could move on to the next thing, not here. It was very different.

The next day, I had a free day as my excursions did not start until the following day. I toured Florence on foot, and I have never walked as much in my life as I did in Italy. I walked everywhere, I downloaded an app on my phone to help me get around, and carried multiple maps with me as the streets were very confusing to me at first when I was there. I saw the most beautiful cathedrals, experienced the most attractive people playing live music on the streets and creating art, I saw some of the most beautiful graffiti everywhere, there was gelato on every corner it seemed, the most beautiful clothing stores, horse drawn carriage rides, carousels in the middle of the town square, it was absolutely glorious!

That first day, I visited a restaurant and met two men from England. We talked about life, and I shared with them how this was my first time traveling to Europe and how nervous I was. They asked me to think about putting my maps away and getting lost on purpose. My jaw dropped, and I said, "Okay, I will, and I did." I got lost and found the one thing I couldn't find on the map the travel agent gave me—a wine and painting class!

This wine and paint class was 60 euros and held in the back of a Chinese restaurant. I dreamed of taking a wine and paint class in the countryside of Italy, and the Universe delivered me something quite different. And it was glorious!

I painted Cyprus trees and grapes with another person who happened to be an exchange student from New York. We had so much fun, laughing, creating, and connecting. It was wild because they were having a rainstorm that night, and we didn't know it because this restaurant did not have windows. We didn't know what was happening until the electricity went out. I was calmer than I ever expected to be. The people who led the class and the restaurant owners lit candles, and we continued painting and connecting. We enjoyed homemade limoncello and popcorn.

When we were done with the class, they rolled up our paintings for us and handed us our canvas along with a certificate. Then, the other participant and I walked back to our lodging together until we went in different directions. I wasn't so scared to be in a foreign country alone anymore. It was glorious!

And that's really where my next phase of my spiritual journey began.

The next day, after a very restful evening, I was over my jet lag and went downstairs for breakfast. It was so delicious, I ate the most wonderful chocolate croissants and lattes. Some of the breakfast items were really odd to me; they had an array of items like mixed cheeses and meats, hard-boiled eggs, waffles, cereals, different breads, and pastries. After breakfast, I was off to my adventures. Every day, I toured many wineries and cooking classes in the most glorious places in Tuscany. I never had been much of a wine person. I discovered while on the winery tours that I wanted to experience Italy like a local, meet local people, and see every ounce of the countryside.

The wineries and castles were how I knew I would experience a part of this. I saw some of the most beautiful trees, flowers, and artichoke plants! I remember being in such awe over seeing them, as I had never seen an artichoke plant before. I hugged many trees, I even stood in the middle of a giant hollow tree while in Cinque Terre, and climbed some of the biggest trees I have ever seen in Ireland! I experienced so much beauty while I was in Europe.

It was amazing that there were gazebos covered in vines, flowers everywhere, and statues in the middle of freeway intersections. I felt like my jaw dropped almost everywhere I was. I was like a 40-plus-year-old kid when I looked at everything, touched everything, and did everything. The many times I felt scared, I remembered to take long, peaceful, deep breaths to get grounded again before I gained the courage to step outside and start the next thing.

One of my favorite things when I was in Italy was when I got to experience cooking in the countryside of Tuscany with about 20 people. It was so beautiful, it was like a storybook. Before entering the building, we walked down a long outside stairway filled with shrubs and flowers. Just to the bottom left of the stairs were a couple of huge brick ovens where we would later bake our pizzas. Then we walked inside a massive kitchen with multiple tables for everyone to eat, and just outside that was another room where all the walls were actually windows overlooking the entire countryside. The countryside had so many beautiful flowers and trees it seemed to go on forever. I had never seen anything like it. This was where we prepared the food we were making together. We made homemade pizza dough and pasta with our hands and a roller, without kitchen machinery! We also made homemade gelato and tiramisu, bruschetta, and roast. It was the most delicious food I had ever eaten! We moved the pizza dough in our hands and flipped it in the air, sang, laughed, connected, and even got cooking certificates!

After about a week of going on adventures before all the other ladies arrived, I was ready to pack up my bags and head to the train station to meet them. I was excited and nervous all at once. Before I left the States, my parents were really nervous for me because I was traveling alone, and my stepmom almost talked me out of going, though I went anyway.

This adventure to Europe was another way for me to heal and grow. It was an all-women daypack retreat that consisted of us day hiking for at least three of the seven days of this journey. We had a driver who took us to the various locations we hiked to and picked us up where we would end the day. We were driven around in a fancy, smaller bus with very comfortable seats that reclined, seat belts, and foot and arm rests. There were many windy roads along the way to every destination that we went to. I was so freaked out by how the cars would drive so close to one another, maybe a foot apart at times, as if they didn't have any fear. I remember being so happy that I didn't have to drive.

Our driver, Roarie, would move our luggage from villa to villa from each town we would stay in. Typically, we would only stay in a town for one evening and move the next day, which aligned with what the trip experience was for me: cherishing every moment. We never knew what was planned for the day until right before our day began. The leaders would prepare us just enough so we would know what we should wear for the day, and gave us a couple of hours to prepare. That time, of course, included us eating our breakfast. This group was called Alchemy Adventures, and their name completely defined the journey of creating whatever we wanted and learning how to truly be present. To live and enjoy every moment, squeeze the juice out of every day, and be deeply grateful for every piece of beauty along the way. The flowers, swing sets, fountains, gazebos, the gardens, the perfect picture spots, dancing in the streets, eating the gelato, the food, the friends I met along the way, the solitude when I needed it, everything, every drop of everything. The trip included food, lodging, and some activities.

While there, I remembered how to take care of myself again, breathe deeply, live in the moment, and cherish every minute of every day.

I smelled the flowers.

I ate the chocolate.

I let the gelato melt in my mouth.

I stood inside a tree, went to parks, danced, let the waves crash all around me, and went on a merry-go-round.

I walked many miles, with wild sheep, cows, horses, and even pet a wild donkey!

I painted for the first time, swung on swing sets, went down slides, twirled, bought sparkly yellow shoes, bought the clothes, created art, journaled, and fell in love with myself.

I sang, connected with people, connected with myself, peed in fields of flowers, hiked some pretty amazing lands, toured a grand coliseum, and pretended I was a performer.

I touched a statue of Juliette's booby because they said it would bring you love.

I got lost on purpose, toured more castles and cathedrals than I can remember, one of which was where they filmed part of "Under the Tuscan Sun."

I danced. I twirled.

I stayed in amazing villas, one of which was where the cast of Twilight stayed!

I walked a long trail with a butterfly on my finger for over 20 minutes!

I laughed, tried on, and bought beautiful clothes and shiny shoes that I usually wouldn't buy, and so happened to be yellow.

I went to the opera, rode a water taxi, and rode a gondola.

I stopped when people on the street were breaking out in song, just listened, and swayed my hips in awe of their talent.

I dressed up.

I enjoyed listening to a bagpipe player dressed in full costume in Ireland. I walked through a labyrinth.

I found treasures, meditated, prayed, went on a see-saw, and went down slides.

At the beginning of my journey to Europe, I felt guilty for being able to take a month and travel to Italy, for leaving a company I had built for 20 years, and spending time with myself. While I was on this journey, that dissipated over time.

After 30 days of being in the moment in a foreign land, the guilt I felt about taking time for myself became a distant emotion. What replaced it was a feeling of peace.

QUICK TIPS FOR HOW TO WORK WITH THE HEARTIST WITHIN YOU

Create stillness within for a minimum of five minutes daily. Some examples of this could be meditation, being in nature, prayer, or immersing yourself in a form of art that calls to you, such as music, art, cooking, journaling, etc. By doing this, all of the busyness of life will be a distant memory, if only for a few minutes every day.

Create time to be truly present with this book for at least 10 minutes daily.

Once you've finished the book, continue to be present with yourself for at least 10 minutes a day.

QUESTIONS & ANSWERS

1.   What do you hope to get out of this experience?

_____

_____

_____

2.   How does it feel connecting to a deeper love within?

_____

_____

_____

3.   Who do you need to let go of or forgive to make more room in your heart for loving yourself?

_____

_____

_____

Journal

CHAPTER 1

LISTEN TO YOUR INTUITION

Asking for signs from the Universe is part of my daily spiritual practice. It has to be.

There was a time in my life when I was upside down in two homes, lost a potential buyer, and depleted my 401 (k) in home renovations to support myself financially. My intuition helped me hold onto my faith and trust in the direction I was going then.

To me, communicating with the Universe the way I do is a part of my faith. Over the years, I've learned that while it's not always easy to have and keep faith, it works best for me when I don't have any attachment to what the final product would look like.

Easier said than done.

Arriving at a place of being unattached feels like one big emotional roller coaster.

And it all started for me when I asked the Universe, "Where is the right and best place for me to live?"

I'll never know why I asked it. At the time, I had three homes. I was living in one, and the other two were rental properties.

I loved my house. It was my dream home—a castle. I didn't want to move, but something deep inside prompted me to ask the question, and I trusted it.

I had everything I needed. And still, it was time for me to go.

I was going through so many emotions regarding letting go of my beautiful house. I had put my heart and soul into every crevice of that home over the past two years. I could look at every area of my home and feel every piece of my heart I put into each item. Everything was intentional. I felt like I was living in a breathing piece of art, and a breathing piece of art that I created with massive intention over the past couple of years.

Before I found Feng Shui, my homes had always revolved around my ex-husband's style or the things my children liked. Nothing was really a reflection of me. And that was a common theme within my home, business, friendships, family, everywhere! It was more comfortable for me to give myself to others by showering them with an abundance of compliments and gifts than for me to value myself.

Giving compliments and gifts is a beautiful expression of appreciation, but I took it to the extreme. The more I did this for others, the more I was hiding from myself without even knowing it. I thought I was such a huge giver when, in all actuality, I was taking from myself and others. It was so hard for me to receive a compliment from others, and I would mostly brush it off.

Over time, my patterns and behaviors left me resentful and depleted, so whenever I returned home for the day, I would go and hide from all that mattered most to me, which were my children. I hid in my room and lost myself in Hollywood magazines, catching up on my TV shows in my room, shopping, decorating, or sleeping, to name a few.

All my children ever wanted from me was quality time with me. They wanted me to listen to them. They needed my time and energy to help with their homework or go on bike rides. They needed me to cook them dinner, listen to them and hear what was happening in their lives, watch a silly movie with them, and go swimming with them. I didn't have time or energy for any of it. All the things I now view as so simple weren't simple for me then.

I was lost then. I gave everything away. I didn't even know what my style was any longer. My style became whatever my man's style was. Conforming to what my man wanted had become easier over the years. And it was precisely what drove them away because as time drew on, I became bored. I did not have a mind of my own; I thought they wanted easy, and my view of easy was me conforming to who I thought they wanted me to be. I would break plans with my friends or family whenever my man wanted me to do something different.

Over time, I found Feng Shui. I simplified this home by decluttering and decorating it. I made it ultra feminine. It became more me over the years. Every piece of furniture was absolutely beautiful. The drapes flowed so softly and were sheer. The windows used to be closed. When I started decluttering, I started every day with open windows. I was so excited for the daylight to shower prisms in my home every day. I had crystals hanging from every window throughout the house. The crystals would have rainbow prisms on multiple walls and even the ceiling. It brought me so much joy to awaken to this every day. I had messages with every object in my home, including uplifting positive sayings.

Everything had meaning in my home. Everything was so incredibly beautiful and welcoming. I fell in love with this home, and I really struggled with awaiting the response the Universe was going to give me as to whether I would stay or go from this castle I now called home. However, I trusted and stood firm in my path. Whatever path the Universe would guide me on is the direction I would go.

It took me about three months to realize that selling my home and moving was the best decision for me. Though the path was windy and emotional, I let it go and began the process of moving my life.

It took about another six months to complete my move. Not only did I need to place the home on the market, but I was also planning my renovations for the home I was moving back into. I also had to wait to begin the renovations until my current tenant moved out. There were so many moving parts and pieces. I definitely needed the time and space to move through all of the emotions and choices that went along with all of that. The most amazing thing I decided to do was truly feel every emotion I was going through. I was so incredibly patient and loving with myself through this entire process.

I leaned into my spiritual practice during this time. I cared for myself deeply, and my self-care practice brought comfort, healing, peace, and love.

Here are 15 tools to use as you develop your ritual practice. I have listed some of these items below with definitions and explanations. I find that when I seek clarity on my path, I should sit in a beautiful location I have created and listen. I have a special space specifically dedicated to what I now call my "zen den" within my home. I created this space with many things that I love. Such as the sound of trickling water from the bubbles in my fish tank, beautiful instruments that have a lovely sound when played, candles, incense, a space to create my art, lots of pillows and cozy blankets, and speakers to play beautiful music. I encourage you to create a beautiful space that is in celebration of the beautiful love that you have for yourself. A place where you will commit to spending time with yourself in your home. Suppose you don't have the space for this to be solely dedicated to you. I find that a special place in nature does the trick for me. It doesn't have to be far from home.

I've learned how to trust my internal compass to guide me. My intuition told me what creative or spiritual practice was going to serve me best. I listened to that internal guidance. I encourage you to do the same. You don't have to use all these tools provided. However, my intention is to give you as many ideas as possible. Maybe you'll connect with one idea. Or you could connect with a few. Ask yourself what would be best for you and trust that message.

Pay attention to resistance and avoidance, as they act as barriers to our heart's message for us.

TOOLS TO HELP YOU DEVELOP YOUR SPIRITUAL PRACTICE

Adventures: I went through many phases of where I would date and times where I chose not to date. One thing that I was determined to do was live my life and experience new things, whether I was dating or not. Trying new things brought me great joy.

If there was something I always wanted to do, I booked it. Sometimes, I bought one ticket, and other times, I bought more. I followed my intuition. I trusted the guidance my heart was calling out to me. I booked painting classes, wine and chocolate festivals, hot air balloon rides, lantern festivals, concerts, plays, horseback rides, game nights, cooking classes, hikes, ziplining, a festival of lights, and charity events, to name a few.

Give yourself permission to try something new. It's perfectly normal to be scared to venture out into a new class or pick up a new hobby. So be gentle and kind to yourself.

List three places in your local area you've always wanted to try/go:

1. _____

2. _____

3. _____

Now, commit to go to one of the three places mentioned above within the next month.

List your date with yourself below.

Date: _____.

Fire Ceremonies: A fire ceremony is a Native American practice that is usually performed every full and new moon. You do not have to wait for a full or new moon in order to do a fire ceremony. Fire Ceremonies are wonderful during a Full or New Moon, when you want to release whatever is binding you and welcome the things you want into your life.

I first learned of fire ceremonies while I was on my journey to becoming a shaman. We were required to try our fire ceremonies around the new and full moons, which happened about every two weeks. I loved performing my fire ceremonies, as they helped me feel at peace every time I conducted one. I learned to love the smell of fire outside and on my clothes because it symbolized healing and transformation to me, which was something that I craved and now created.

Fire ceremonies need a little preparation and mastery. Look for Full Moon gatherings in your local area. Many spiritual centers offer them and can work with you to release and welcome in a safe environment during their fire ceremony.

Research spiritual centers in your local area that offer Moon and/or Fire ceremonies. List them below with their contact information.

1. _____

2. _____

3. _____

Sand Paintings: The Sand Painting has been used around the world for self-healing. It's one of the most powerful energy medicine tools. I can't champion it enough, or say enough about this divine energy medicine tool. I use them all the time in my personal spiritual practices and also when being of service to others. With the right intentions and a commitment from you, it holds the power to transform issues and transmute energies in your life in a matter of days or weeks, as opposed to months or years without it.

To create your Sand Painting, you'll want to find an area of your life that you are not at peace with. To help you identify what area of your life you're going to create a Sand Painting on, here are questions to consider.

1.   Is there someone you have been procrastinating on forgiving?
2.   Is there anger or sadness you are holding onto?
3.   Is there something you really want to welcome into your life?

Create an intention, something that you do want. Find a private spot in your yard where animals or home vendors will not disturb it during the three days you will assemble it. Gather beautiful objects in nature that you can release back into nature once your Sand Painting is complete in three days. This piece is very important as Mother Earth will take on whatever is left once the ceremony is complete. Begin your three-day Sand Painting journey as detailed below in Creating Your Sacred Circle.

The Sand Painting is made from objects from nature that symbolize different aspects of your life. Each item you pick up, you either blow into it what you want to release or welcome in. It is important that you pick items that can be dispersed in nature once your Sand Painting ceremony is complete. As you build your painting, send it positive thoughts, feelings, and emotions. Set a positive intention and breathe. The more energy, intention, and feeling you transfer into your piece, the more healing energy it holds.

I encourage you to visit your Sand Painting as often as you like during the three days. Observe it, meditate with it, journal, move objects inside of it around, add new items. However, do not remove your objects until the end of the third day when the ceremony is complete. If items blow outside of your Sand Painting during this time do not place them back in as this is a message that it has already been released.

You will do this for a total of three days. On the third day, it is time to release all items back into nature.

It's one of my favorite healing tools. Make it what you want. It can be one piece of memorabilia or a complex, woven piece of art. Eventually, it will become a representation of your life.

Chakra Balancing: Chakra balancing is believed to align the flow of energy in the body, much as a tune-up fixes a car to operate at peak efficiency. It's based on the ancient belief that our body has seven energy centers and can work within to harmonize them all.

There are multiple ways that this can be done. Sometimes I had other people do this for me, and there were times when I did it on my own. Every time this was completed I felt realigned and at peace.

To balance your chakras, I encourage you to create a beautiful ceremony in the bath, shower or a body of water. Bring oils, flowers, candles, and healing music. As you cleanse your body imagine washing away anything that is unbalanced in you and your chakras and see them as balanced and flowing beautifully. It is encouraged to drink lots of water before and after this ceremony and get lots of rest.

Journaling: generally involves the practice of keeping a diary or journal that explores thoughts and feelings surrounding the events of your life.

There are many different forms of journaling. Typically, I would handwrite my journals, as I learned that writing in my journal instead of typing connects me more to what I am writing. There were times when I would journal with my non-dominant hand as I learned that this connected me to my inner child. There were also times when I would journal by drawing pictures that would come to me, and oftentimes shortly after I drew my picture with pencils and other forms of media, it would come to life in my experiences.

There were times when I would read a daily meditation from an inspirational book and journal my understanding of it and how I would apply it to my life. This was so freeing and helped me connect to myself and what was important to me at the time.

If you've never journaled before, I invite you to start in a deeply sacred space by writing a letter to yourself on a clean piece of paper. Tell yourself what you're proud of, grateful for, and looking forward to next.

If you're familiar with journaling, I invite you to try something new. If you've never tried journaling with your non-dominant hand, give it a go. It will move you out of your head and into your heart.

Another option is called Automatic Writing. This is a technique that a lot of people use. Don't think about what you're writing or what's pouring out of you. Just write. Let it flow.

Below is an example of how to perform an Automatic Writing Session:

On a clean piece of paper, write:

Dear God, Dear Guides, Dear Universe, of the highest compassion and love. Thank you for revealing to me what I need to know. Thank you for writing through me.

Afterward, meditate for 10 minutes.

If you don't feel anything come up, rewrite the sentences:

Thank you for revealing to me what I need to know. Thank you for writing through me.

Go back into a meditative state for a few minutes. When you feel/sense/think new thoughts, capture them on paper. Don't think, judge, or doubt yourself. Just write. When your handwriting changes, you're channeling and doing Automatic Writing.

Daily Meditations: are a very common practice to help create a deeper connection to self. Meditation helps calm the inner critic by creating stillness throughout the day.

There are many different kinds of meditation. You can start your day with a quiet prayer.

Mindfulness meditation, visualization, and even walking meditation are common practices nowadays. There are so many different apps and even social media influencers that offer guided meditations for free. I suggest committing to a meditation practice and starting small. Find a guided meditation that resonates with you and commit to doing this every day for a minimum of one minute for 90 days.

When I first started meditating, it was difficult for me to sit still and hard in a quiet state of mind. Here are steps that helped me as I deepened my meditation practice.

1. Block off time on your calendar for you to connect to your inner self.
2. Find a silent space where you will be uninterrupted for a minimum of one minute.

3. Find a guided meditation that you connect to.
4. Journal in your own way any messages that you received during your meditation.

Hiking: I found hiking to be so incredibly grounding and freeing. I remember when I was younger, I dreaded hiking. After I went to Italy, that changed. We hiked at least half of the time I was there, and our hikes would last a minimum of six miles and sometimes up to 13 miles. After returning from Italy, I would hike as often as possible; hiking helped me connect with Mother Nature and find my inner peace. Hiking cured my anxiety. I started carrying a backpack instead of a purse and always had clothes to change into for hiking in the back of my car. I loved being in nature and connecting with trees, animals, flowers, and everything else about it. The more I hiked, the more I could see and feel the stories nature would tell as I walked the desired paths.

Get curious about the state you live in. Research some of the best hiking spots in your area online or through local apps. You can look up hikes based on the type of terrain you're looking for and the difficulty level you're interested in. Ask friends if they would join you for a hike this week. I would encourage you to find a friend to hike with who is already familiar with the trail, or select a trail that is well populated with people and markers along the way to help you stay on the path. If neither option is available, state or national parks are great as they will provide maps of the trails for a small fee, and some have guided trails with the ranger.

Create a Vision Board: Schedule some time with yourself or with a small group of friends to create your vision boards. If you're unsure how to get started, look up events in your area, as vision board parties are very popular now.

If you're creating a vision board with friends, I suggest you ask everyone to bring their favorite magazines, scissors, tape, and poster boards so you don't have to provide the materials. Make it a fun pot-luck as creating a vision board can take some time.

Put on some beautiful music and light some candles to help set the perfect mood for creating your visions and dreams. Set an intention for what you are creating, and be open to the unexpected and miracles.

Set a timer for two hours to collect the images and words that you connect with, and then take a small break to refresh your mind. When you come back from your break, I encourage you to set the timer again for another two hours.

Once your timer goes off, it is now time to place the images on your poster board. The placement of these words and pictures is key. A vision board is a piece of art representing experiences and things you call into life. It's important to have images and words on the board that showcase emotion, color, things, and places you want to manifest. It's sort of like a puzzle you are creating and customizing to get clear on what you're drawn to create in your life. Don't forget to sign and date your vision board.

After everyone completes their vision board, take some time for each person to share the story of what they created. Lastly, place your vision board in a space where you will see it daily.

For extra bonus points, set aside some time in the coming week to write the story of your vision board and tape it to the back side of the vision board.

Gratitude: I learned that being grateful for everything in my life gives the universe the signal to show me things to be grateful for. I have always been a very grateful person. My parents raised me to be grateful for everything, though. Ugh, I didn't understand the power that gratitude held when I was young. I didn't know what it meant to feel grateful from every ounce of my being, day after day, until I began practicing it altogether for 30 days.

The more sincere I am about my gratitude, and the deeper I feel my gratitude in my body, the more it shows up on my path for me to be grateful for.

To help deepen your gratitude practice, try this exercise.

For at least seven days, begin each day by saying, "Thank you for this beautiful, new day." Each evening before going to bed, write a minimum of three things you are grateful for in your gratitude journal.

Some examples of this are as follows.

1. I am so happy and grateful for yesterday's beautiful hike I took with my friend. There were so many beautiful mountains surrounding us, and in the middle of our hike, we saw this beautiful white boulder that we all became very curious about and had to touch it. It was so far away from where we were when we saw it. When we did, one of my friends said, "Stacie, there is a small trail that leads up to the white boulder." I was so happy to not only touch the boulder, but have my picture taken so that I can look at it as a reminder of the beautiful day of connection with my friends, nature, and me! Thank you, thank you, thank you!

2. With all of my heart, thank you for the beautiful sunset I experienced while driving home from work. The mountains lit up as the sun went down, and the perfect song was playing on the radio while I watched this beauty. Thank you, thank you, thank you!

After completing your gratitude list, read each one out loud for extra BONUS points.

Create your very own dance party!: I learned to move my body with the sound of music in any way my body wanted to. I have always loved to dance. As my kids were growing up, I would "mom dance" around the kitchen and get them to dance with me, and at times, I would pick up my little dogs and dance with them. It always brought me so much joy and to a place where I felt free.

I encourage you to dedicate one day a week to creating a dance party for yourself with a song that lights you UP. If you find this is hard to do in your regular attire, create your very own character and dance!

For extra BONUS points invite other friends to join your dance party. You can create a live video and share it with the social media world. I promise you this will inspire others to dance along with you and you could double dog dare others to create their own dance party to share with others too! PEOPLE LOVE FUN!

Connect With People You Love: For most of my life, I have done things alone. Connection was a vulnerable and intimate place for me to be. It taught me how to deepen my trust, communication, partnership, and courage. It also helped me see the power in two or more like-minded individuals focused on a common goal.

List all of the things you love to do and set up a friend date to do something you both enjoy. Or create your own event at home. This is a great way to practice surrender and trusting the unfolding of the unknown.

Pay attention to how you feel in your body when you're doing something new. Ask yourself if you feel alive, or are you having fun? Are you in resistance because you're uncomfortable or scared because it's new? Remember that your ego wants to keep you safe and comfortable, and your soul wants to live life out loud and experience everything.

Get in the Kitchen and Cook!: I grew to love creating art and saw cooking as another art form. I found it therapeutic and courageous because I never knew how things would turn out. I began to make different dishes. I would crave something new and risky to make, and look up a recipe online or in one of my recipe books that I had never tried before. During this time, I tested recipes out on friends and family. People could feel the love I put into every bite. And, it warmed me up from the inside out, helping me feel deep love and gratitude.

Write down a recipe you've always wanted to try below.

_____

_____

_____

_____

TITLE:

INGREDIENTS

DIRECTIONS

Cleansing the Home: The purpose of cleansing energy from your home is to release old, stagnant or even low vibrational energy from the house and welcome new, aligned, intentional energy to best support you. There are many ways to cleanse your home, and practitioners in your area who can support you if you don't feel comfortable doing this alone.

A couple of methods I have used over the years to cleanse my home are ringing a feng shui bell throughout my home, sound healing recordings, smudging, and a feng shui salt cleanse. They all create the same result because they intend to help neutralize the potentially negative effects in any home or office and welcome in the highest possible energy.

Here's a description of the salt cleanse method I've used.

I would buy sea salt in bulk. Many retailers sell sea salt in big quantities. I'd buy a 25-pound bag. Next, buy small disposable cups and count the corners in your home. Don't forget the closets, bathrooms, garage or any area of your property you use a lot. You'll want to put a cup in every corner of every room in your home. Line up the cups on a tray and add three tablespoons of sea salt to each cup.

Have a clear intention of what you want to release from your home and what you welcome in. As you place a cup of salt in each corner of every room of your home, repeat your intention out loud or quietly to yourself.

You'll want to leave the cups sit for three days. At the end of the three days, pick up all of the cups and flush the salt down every drain throughout the home that is closest to each cup, including toilets. Then dispose of the cups.

Practice cleansing your home at least monthly or as often as you feel necessary. A great way to add beautiful new energy into a home is to purchase a beautiful bouquet of flowers or a plant and place it on the table for all to see and experience the beauty together.

Mandala: These beautiful creations are a sacred therapeutic method for me. They help me move out of my mind and drop down into my heart. I let the mandala design guide me. I take my time and don't overthink what color is being used next. I've used mandalas in my healing journey for decades. There are no defined rules for mandala drawings. Every Mandala has symmetry. Let your creativity flow and enjoy the process.

Art: helped me to connect to my femininity. I first learned how to paint when I went to Italy a few months after I retired. I was relaxed and at peace. I loved being surrounded by the beauty of Italy and stumbled across an art class where I painted grapevines, cypress trees and a vineyard freelance. After returning home, I craved to learn more about art and headed to the perfect place, my sister-in-law's home in Colorado. While I was there, I learned how to do a new type of art for me, which was called mixed media. It used canvas, different types of beautiful paper, markers, pencils, paint, chalk, fabric, and accessories. She taught me how to make my first angel. I learned this by watching her videos, art books, and online images of angels created with mixed media. I was surprised by how beautiful my art was with no training whatsoever. I loved art. One of my favorite parts was that if I didn't like something, I painted over it.

Over the years, I have learned how much of my artwork is connected to my heart. That's why I call everything The Heartist Journey. What we create from our hearts will look different than what we create from our minds.

QUESTIONS & ANSWERS

1. What spiritual practices listed in this chapter feel most aligned with you today?

_____

_____

_____

2. Write out how it feels when you connect to your intuition?

_____

_____

_____

3. What other spiritual modalities work for you?

_____

_____

_____

4. What's one thing you'll incorporate into your morning routine based on what you've learned in this chapter?

_____

_____

_____

5. What's one thing you'll incorporate into your evening routine based on what you read in this chapter?

_____

_____

_____

Journal

_____

_____

_____

_____

_____

_____

_____

_____

_____

_____

_____

_____

_____

_____

CHAPTER 2

FENG SHUI

O NE OF THE MOST PROFOUND PRACTICES THAT CRACKED ME open was Feng Shui. It's an ancient Chinese practice that helps us create harmony and balance in our lives.

And when Feng Shui entered my reality shortly after my medicine wheel training, I knew my life was about to change again.

The timing was perfect.

The road to creating a healthy, happy family was a journey I did not have any premeditated plans for. I had no idea the length of time this journey would take, nor did I have any idea how it would all unfold. I just knew it was time.

Our family had been "existing" for a very long time, and I came to Earth for more than that. I came here to thrive and knew I was meant to create big, beautiful things for myself and with my family.

Right before I found Feng Shui, my son needed some support.

I was desperate to find the solution to help him on his journey. I remember being on my hands and knees, weeping to God for the first time in many years. I asked him for help to find the right and perfect place for my son, to help him find love and peace within himself. I needed help for him, and in that moment, I realized I also needed help for me. What I wanted for him, I also wanted for me. To find the love inside me, for me, the way that I loved others.

We both went on personal development programs to manage my energy through my growth, and all the feelings that came to the surface, I did what I knew best. I avoided it altogether. Instead, I de-cluttered the house.

It was a perfect storm of energy, feeling, and decor. I was always fond of decorating, and until then, I viewed Feng Shui as a decorating practice.

I contacted a local Feng Shui master, who became my guru for the time being. I soaked up everything from her like a sponge.

I immersed myself in the healing aspect of Feng Shui and its balancing benefits, and over the next months and years, I truly became a believer in it.

During our first phone call, she asked me about my goals for the next year. My answer was simple and clear. I wanted balance in every aspect of my life. She introduced me to the bagua chart, and we began to balance out my life.

It seemed as if the more I decluttered, the stronger my intuition became. We spoke about everything I wanted in my life: clarity on my life's purpose, supportive, loving friends and family, my right man, a healthy, happy family, optimal health, money, balance in every area of my life, and much more.

Once we scheduled our first appointment for this next piece of my journey, the energy clearing had already started, and all the things I wanted in my life began shifting into being. At the end of our call, we scheduled our first in-person appointment. It was her first appointment of the New Year. I was honored and excited to begin this journey that would come to be a journey that would continue for the rest of my life.

Leading up to my Feng Shui master coming to my home, I was so excited about everything I wanted to come into being that I spent every moment I had decluttering. I went through every drawer, cabinet, closet, piece of furniture in my home, and every nook and cranny. No stones were left unturned.

While decluttering my home, I found some pretty crazy things. I examined every piece of furniture and really thought about its purpose in my life. Did I love it? If not, it went into a donate, sell, or throw-away pile.

I filled up my extended single-car garage with items I was donating or throwing away so fast that I was running out of space. As I decluttered, I began giving away clothes, nick-nacks, and furniture to friends and family. They absolutely loved it, and so did I.

I was constantly in awe of how much I had acquired over the years. I had brand new dressers in the closets. I had duplicate pieces of furniture all over my home and shook my head in disbelief, wondering what was going through my head when I continued buying things over the years, when I had more than I could ever need or want. I had forgotten how many things I had because I would tuck them away in closets that had become virtually empty over the years since I was divorced and my children moved out of the house. It was crazy, as my house was always very tidy and neat. The excess items and furniture that were placed in closets were out of sight and, oddly enough, very clean inside the closets too. I had so many nice things. Everyone loved it when I went through my decluttering over the years because my trash became their treasures.

Our first in-person consultation was amazing. She had so much knowledge of Feng Shui. We walked through my entire house, and she gave me guidance as to what should go where. I carried around a stash of blank Post-it notes and would quickly write down whatever she said and pop those suckers on the walls as we walked through the house together. This was brilliant as she was like a walking textbook of Feng Shui.

She patiently helped me see the items in my home that reflected the exact opposite of the love and harmony I wanted to experience in my life.

I had always wanted to share my life with my lifelong mutually exclusive romantic partner, have deep relationships with my friends and family, and live a passionate life, and my house did not reflect that at the time.

I had shared examples of items I found as I decluttered. I was shocked at the things I had kept and didn't remember putting them there.

I tucked away my wedding rings and other jewelry from my past two marriages in a cabinet. One of them is a set of little candle holders from my honeymoon night on my first marriage. In another cranny, I found my wedding rings and other jewelry from my second marriage. They were tucked away so safely that I even forgot they were there.

These two finds were particularly interesting for me. For years, I said I wanted to attract my right and perfect man into my life. I was in a romantic relationship at the time that I believed was the right fit for me.

And yet, how could true love happen in my life if I were holding onto pieces of past love? It couldn't. I was unknowingly and still energetically blocking my path to new love. I ended up selling my beautiful jewelry from my ex-husband so I could create the space for my right man to come in.

My Feng Shui master pointed out that I had at least 10 pictures in my house of single women who looked very sad and alone. I had one huge picture right on the outside of my bedroom door, at least 6 feet tall by 4 feet wide, of a naked woman sitting down with her back and the side of her face looking down with a blanket draped over her.

That was one of many images of women I had throughout my house. At the time, I had no images of a woman and a man in a loving embrace or laughing in my entire house, not a single one. All but maybe five of the 50 pieces of art throughout my house were fairly dark and sad. I had never realized it before my Feng Shui master came into my life.

This was a huge aha moment for me that helped me see exactly where I was at in attracting men who were emotionally unavailable in my life because that was who I was, too. I was not open at all to letting anyone in. My house reflected exactly who I was at the time, and that was very sad and alone.

My home was beautiful, and friends always commented on how my house resembled a model home.

My Feng Shui master learned how much I loved vision boards and how it was an important part of my journey. Her method of Feng Shui was Western and used a chart called the Bagua and she compared it to a vision board.

She said, "We are going to create your home as a vision board through Feng Shui."

She handed me a Bagua chart with nine squares. Each square symbolized a different area of life: children and creativity, spirituality, romance, helping people and travel, career, family, health, fame and reputation, and wisdom.

Western Feng Shui balances the entire home's energy by decorating and designing the areas of the Bagua chart to flow. The more I learned about the Bagua the more I knew I needed to keep seeing my practitioner to guide me because there are so many pieces to it.

I was ready to create an atmosphere that would draw harmony and love into my life. More importantly, I was ready to receive it.

Over the next year, my Feng Shui master came to my home at least 20 times. She was a huge part of my journey and gave me so many nuggets of gold. I was salivating the entire time.

I learned so much from her.

Months into my journey of Feng Shuiing my home, I noticed how much different my life looked. My life was changing for the positive at a rapid pace. I had direction. I knew exactly what I wanted. I was feeling happier. I was sleeping better, and so much more. I knew Feng Shui was changing my life for the better. If my atmosphere felt better, I would feel better and I would attract better into my life. I wanted to spread what I learned to others, so I also began to incorporate the Bagua into my office outside of my home.

Decluttering was so time-consuming that it could have been a part-time job for me. The practice of Feng Shui states that as we release things that no longer serve us, we make room for more that does.

My home at the time was 6,000 square feet, and it took me nearly two years to Feng Shui and declutter.

It was unbelievable as I decluttered and Feng Shuied people. Things would either move out of my life, or new people and things would appear. Of course, some stayed in my life, too.

Some I was okay with, and some I didn't like letting go of. And I knew it all was necessary in the deepest parts of me and followed the flow. There were times when I held on longer than I should have because the longer I held on, the more pain I would feel.

In time, I understood that I had to let go of some things to create the space to welcome all that I desired into my life.

It was difficult keeping up with the rapid pace of changes occurring in my life on every level, but that's been the pace I've kept most of my life.

I'm an "all or nothing" kinda woman. Everything I do, I tend to go "all in" once I commit to something. Decluttering was no exception to the rule of life.

There's nothing like a new practice to teach us about our shadow side. I had always thought I was a tidy person. Once I learned the art of decluttering, I saw things I didn't see before about my personality.

I would hide things—feelings, situations, stuff. Whatever we experience in our inner world is a reflection of our outer world. And if I were hiding items in the nooks and crannies of my home, I was doing it in my heart, in my personal life, professional life, family life, and probably even my office.

The clutter I found in my home symbolized my life. On the outside, everything looked great. And yet, hidden beneath the surface was more energetic clutter than I could ever imagine.

Feng Shui helped me see that, and shift it. When I changed the external, the internal followed. It seemed the faster I decluttered my home, the more my life changed.

With each piece of furniture, nic-nac, or clothing I released, I could feel the energy of the home shift. I truly believed I was making space in my life to receive everything I had ever wanted.

"This or something better," I would say.

The further I went down this journey, the more intense it became, which is true for any transition. The clearer I became about what I wanted in my life, the cleaner the energy in my home became, and the more things in my house and personal life broke apart.

My refrigerator broke. I found a beehive just outside of my son's bathroom that I could hear through the vents. Windows malfunctioned. One of my pool pumps broke. Shrubs died, and on and on.

It felt like everything was falling apart, literally and figuratively, when, in reality, it was falling into place to create space for something better.

The romantic relationship I had been in for four years ended a few months into this process. My family was going through a deep transformation, individually and together. I began to lose passion for the career and the company I had been in for the past 20 years. I lost my appetite, friendships ended, and new ones emerged. I felt like I was dying, and I was because I let go of the things that no longer aligned with what I was inviting into my life. My new way of being emerged with many new people, places, and things.

At some point, I added a cleansing ceremony to this journey. Some of the salt crystallized, and some cups had dead tiny black bugs around the shelf where I placed them.

I cleansed the space monthly after that.

The more I did this, the more the people in my life changed. I was so committed to this new way of life that it spilled over into my office space, and within a few years, I was supporting other people's aspirations of bringing Feng Shui into their homes and lives as well.

Over the years, the people I helped declutter and decorate with the foundation of Feng Shui had big wins. My friend manifested her husband. Another friend had a lawsuit dismissed, and a couple of huge business deals came through, equivalent to close to a million dollars. A third friend manifested a couple of hundred thousand dollars.

Feng Shui became a way of life for me.

The more I practiced all of these things, the more in tune I became with myself, which helped me gain clarity about what was most important to me in life and what path was next for me.

I found my passions: partnership, love, connection, and relationships. I found all of this while exploring new things or things I had already practiced. After furthering my art skills, I was able to reintroduce hobbies into my life and take them to the next level. I practiced my passions with others and alone. I learned what made me tick and how to follow my bliss.

When I follow the path of least resistance, I always end up exactly where I am supposed to be at the right time and space.

QUICK TIPS

Decluttering or creating space in the home or office is the most significant part of Feng Shui. If we have clutter in our environment, we have clutter somewhere in our lives. Here are some ways to begin the decluttering process. Decluttering creates the space to receive what you truly want to create in your life.

1. It's important to first get clear on what you want to create in your life.
2. Take some time to meditate on what you want in your life, and bring a journal with you.
3. Write down the items that come to you during meditation no matter how outrageous or out of range they seem to be.
4. Begin by decluttering the items and areas of your space that may be the least sentimental to you. Often, this could mean starting with your closet.
5. Create five separate piles
    a. A pile of throw-away items
    b. A pile of giveaway items
    c. A pile of items to keep
    d. A pile of items to fix
    e. A pile of things to sell
6. Keep organized with your piles in each room or space you move onto next in order to avoid creating new clutter along the way.
7. Drink lots of water during this process and rest when you feel you need it. You are moving a lot of energy, and it's important to listen to your body and give it what it needs.
8. Once completed, all spaces celebrate you and all that you accomplished.

9. It's important to repeat this process a minimum of twice per year to keep your environment in the flow of receiving.
10. Find a Feng Shui practitioner who practices either Western or Classical in your area to support you in this process.

QUESTIONS AND ANSWERS

1. How is your home a reflection of your personal and professional life?

_____

_____

_____

2. Where can you start decluttering in your home today?

_____

_____

_____

3. How would you describe the energy in your perfect home?

_____

_____

_____

4. What three things do you feel you can let go of today?

_____

_____

_____

Journal

_____

_____

_____

_____

_____

_____

_____

_____

_____

_____

_____

_____

_____

CHAPTER 3

MY COMPANION, WILLIAM

Feng Shui even supported me as I was finally able to grieve the passing of William, my beloved Coton de Tulear. It had been nearly two years since his death. When he died, I was too busy sorting through my family issues to feel and deal with his loss.

As I concluded my decluttering portion of Feng Shui for my home, my beautiful butler pantry was my last room to clear out and organize. It was a room I rarely entered when I lived in this home. As I walked in through the door, I found framed images of William, his dog collar and ashes. And in this little space of my home, I was overcome with very heavy emotions around William's passing.

Clearing the clutter in my house gave me great room in my heart and life to feel what I needed. And William's death was one of those pieces.

Up until that point in my feng shui experience, I was able to deal with the deep emotions that came up as I purged. But this, finding

Williams' belongings, completely caught me off guard. I was surprised at how deeply I felt him in the butler pantry because it was a room I was barely ever in. And never a room he and I were in together. But the grief I had been ignoring for years finally found me.

I held his dog collar in my hands and rubbed my finger over his little silver heart-shaped custom-engraved name tag. While standing in my butler pantry, I allowed myself to deeply feel all of the emotions that were coming up for me in the moment: the pain, sadness, anger, regret, gratitude, love, and joy for all that William brought to my life and my family's life.

He was always so full of life. He was the perfect mixture of playing, loving, and snuggling. He consistently gave so much love to whoever he encountered. William was full of the sweetest energy. He had the underbite that only a mother would love. His imperfect smile made him all that much more lovable to me. I missed him so very much and wanted him to be there with me now, but at the same time, I was so grateful for who he was on my journey.

Hours passed, and I couldn't leave the pantry. And in those hours, I gave myself an incredible gift to fully feel through and experience all the emotions I had repressed for so long. Finally, grieving William was just the springboard to a gateway of healing my body craved.

He gave me a final gift that afternoon. Grieving him forced me to acknowledge my feelings and sit in the pain and discomfort of all the emotions that were flowing through me that I had avoided for it felt like my entire life, specifically the ones I denied most. It wasn't just William that I needed to feel and heal from. Through mourning my beloved William, I was able to see that I needed to clear energetic attachments to my past.

I took a few deep breaths, and when I exhaled, it was like a floodgate opened. Memories poured in—not just of him, but of every role I had played in my life. The single mother, the provider, the protector.

The one who carried it all, never stopping long enough to feel the weight of it. Until now.

As the emotions surfaced, I realized how much forgiveness I had been avoiding. Forgiveness of others, yes—but more than anything, forgiveness of myself. I had to lean into the pain, not push it away. I had to allow myself to feel it all in order to finally let go.

And what came up for me to face, release, and forgive was astounding. It just kept on coming up. I heard names, saw faces, thought of memories I suppressed. As something came up, I felt it, forgave it, and let it go. Like a to-do list, I was purging old pain one by one.

WHAT I FACED, RELEASED, AND FORGAVE

- Painful words from past lovers—the ones that stayed long after they left.
- The failed marriages, the relationships that I had poured everything into, only to watch them fall apart.
- The way I isolated myself, convinced that distance was the only way to protect my heart.
- Control I held onto so tightly—making all the money, paying for everything—choosing men who needed me so I could never feel powerless.
- Heartbreaking truth that even when I was in relationships, I was still alone in parenting. I chose partners who had no interest in raising children, perhaps because I had convinced myself I didn't deserve that kind of support.
- The disconnect with my mother—our relationship was built on control, judgment, and anger, when all I ever longed for was love and acceptance.

- The absence of my father, leaving behind wounds of abandonment that shaped how I moved through the world.
- The fractured relationships with my siblings, a reflection of a childhood where connection was very superficial at best.
- The way my entire identity became wrapped in my business, a relentless pursuit of success that came at the expense of the people I loved most—my children, my partners, and myself.
- The way I saw myself: unworthy, not enough, never enough.
- The way I treated myself: neglected, abandoned, controlled, and sabotaged.
- The way I numbed myself with work, filling every moment with busyness so I wouldn't have to feel the pain and loneliness.

Then, there was a pause in the floodgate of memories, emotions, and people. I took the time to breathe, exhale, and recover some composure for a bit. As I moved my body around and stretched my arms above my head, a scene from one of the hardest moments of my life flashed through my head—when I almost gave my daughter up for adoption. I had picked the family, planned everything, and convinced myself that she deserved better. I was broke, in an abusive relationship, and certain that I wasn't enough.

I sat in the pantry, drawing my knees up to my chest. I squeezed my arms around my legs and rocked back and forth. I allowed myself to visualize the day I gave birth. I held my daughter in my arms. I felt her love. I remembered the feeling of choosing parenthood—motherhood—and the determination to do whatever it was going to take.

I let that scene play over in my head and forgave myself for almost giving her up. And within an instant, things I had held at bay for decades came pouring through my mind.

- The emotional and physical abuse I endured from lovers.
- The molestation when I was ten.
- The way I overextended myself for others, pouring into them while leaving myself empty.
- The way I gave endlessly—money, time, love—trying to prove my worth through what I could offer instead of who I was. I had spent my life taking care of everyone else, convinced that this was the only way I could be valuable. But now, as I was face-to-face with my truth, I realized I had abandoned myself. And I couldn't do that anymore.

Once I let myself process and feel such deep old pain, a very clear message washed over me.

For the first time, I gave myself permission to rest, nourish my body, not just my mind, sleep without guilt, feel without fear, and finally, finally, begin the journey of healing—not just for my children, not just for my past, but for me.

This was the reckoning.

This was the beginning of something new.

I had spent my life building everyone else up—pouring into them, supporting them, making sure they had what they needed—while slowly, silently, depleting myself. I forgot my own worth, lost sight of the value I brought, and instead measured myself by what I could give.

I gave endlessly. To my children. To my friends. To my family. To my employees.

I thought love meant overextending, that my worth was tied to what I could offer rather than who I was. And in the process, I abandoned myself.

Now, with my awareness heightened and my emotional healing underway, a new truth surfaced—my physical health had been suffering, too. Years of exhaustion, running on empty, always putting myself last had taken their toll.

I could no longer ignore it. It was time to care for my body like I was learning to care for my soul.

I needed rest.

I needed nourishment.

I needed to finally give to myself what I had spent a lifetime giving to everyone else.

This, too, was part of my healing.

So much forgiveness took place that day on the floor of my butler pantry. Massive waves of emotion came over me, out of, through me. And by the end of it, I was exhausted, grateful, and tired. The more I leaned into my emotions, the more I could fully experience everything I needed to feel to forgive and heal my deeply seeded wounds from the past.

I realized that I spent years running around taking care of everyone else. Now that my awareness was raised and I was on the path of healing my emotional health, I was experiencing that my physical health had been suffering as well. I decided it was due time to begin the journey of taking care of my physical being, too. I needed sleep. I needed nourishment.

The deeper I was willing to go, the more I was able to express and heal. It was a beautiful exercise in self-love—and one I wasn't expecting to have in the butler's pantry. But I kept searching for love in memories and experiences where I knew love didn't exist. I wanted to see the past for what it was, knowing that the more I could embrace it and forgive it, the deeper I'd love and accept myself.

Since practicing Feng Shui, I have learned that letting go of the past means accepting it as it happened and no longer having any attachments to it. The more I released, the freer I became. I came to realize that the decluttering aspect of Feng Shui was the most powerful piece for me. It became a practice of awareness, forgiveness, and clarity. It helped me release attachments I had lovingly and gratefully so that I could welcome in and truly receive what I wanted next.

FORGIVENESS EXERCISE

1. Are there any people, places, or things with whom you continue to have the same experience? It could be a conversation about a story involving a situation that has been on repeat for weeks, months, or even years on end. Perhaps you're even sick and tired of talking about it, though you can't seem to break the pattern.

2. I invite you to write a list of the people in these stories and the title of the story they are connected to.

3. Set some time aside.

4. Get a pad of paper and a pen. I find that hand writing for this exercise is extremely powerful.

5. For extra credit write with your non-dominant hand. It may seem uncomfortable or foreign at first, though the exercise will keep you present, and possibly help you tap into your inner child.

6. Begin writing a letter to that person, place or experience, referencing what you forgive them for in detail. Then, move on to thanking them in detail for the gifts they brought you. These could be things you learned from them that you do not want to have in your life, and things they helped you realize that you do want. Lastly, ask them to forgive you for any part you played in the experience.

7. Read your letter out loud. Let the emotions flow through as you read the letter.

8. Create a ceremony to release the letter in love. Turn on some ceremonial music, tear up each piece of paper you just read aloud, and disperse the pages. I have used an outside fire pit or drenched in a bucket of water.

9. Repeat this exercise for as many people, places, and things as you desire until you feel complete.

Journal

_____

_____

_____

_____

_____

_____

_____

_____

_____

_____

_____

_____

_____

_____

CHAPTER 4

THE SUMMER OF 2013

THE SUMMER OF 2013 WAS VERY EMOTIONAL FOR ME. I SOLD MY 20-year-old business in the medical records management field. Since getting divorced two years earlier, all my spare time went to personal development.

When I invested in my own growth, I experienced one major lesson after another. And as soon as one finished, it seemed like another lesson was just around the corner waiting for me to explore it.

Everything impacted me emotionally, which left me tired a lot of the time. Despite my tiredness, I kept on going and kept digging to open up and better understand myself.

Instead of numbing out by overworking like I had done for years, watching television, or shopping, I used my time and energy on things that expanded my mind, body, and spirit.

The 2013 Stacie was a woman who attended various classes, seminars, sound healing meditations, workshops, weekly and sometimes bi-weekly coaching sessions. The coaches I invested in were abundant. I had multiple coaches, therapists, or healers helping me bust through the past hurts and pains. I learned something very foreign to me at this time: to ask for and receive support, instead of going back to what was familiar or doing it on my own. I learned that in order to grow more, I needed to learn what was so foreign to me, support.

I was feeling on deeper levels than I had ever allowed myself to feel in my life. I was more open than I had ever been before, I was practicing every day on being present, and I was barely watching television or movies anymore. I had done a lot of work over the years to heal myself, and so much so that I started to see how my family life truly was. My family life had become so unhealthy over the years. The bond mothers have with their children was something I didn't cultivate when my kids were young. I wanted to connect and bond with my children during their upbringing, but I was a partner in a multi-million-dollar company and had no time to add anything to my plate. And sometimes, that included parenting responsibility.

As a young single mom, with kids, and a successful business, I knew I needed help, so I began hiring people. I researched and hired agencies to help me find a nanny to support my kids with after-school activities, feeding them dinner, and tidying up the house. I also enrolled them in tutor programs that helped them understand the subjects they struggled with on a deeper level. Next, I hired gardeners, a pool company, and housekeepers to help me care for our home.

As an older woman in my own healing, I knew why I didn't have as close a relationship with my children as I wanted. I also knew I needed to learn how to love and appreciate myself before I could work on my relationship with the kids. Finally, I learned how to know my value and worth. My mind was awakened, and I finally understood how to connect with myself. It took me until my 40s, but I did it!

My children were now in their 20s, and I had already had my opportunity to raise them. I thought to myself, how can I make up for lost time? What is my path? My answer was that since I could not go back in time, I could move forward, forgive myself, and start over. And that is just what I did.

During the summer of 2013, I was awake enough to see my children in a very dark space. They didn't live much of a life—they were just existing. I thought I had given them everything they needed, but they didn't want "things." They wanted me.

I took responsibility for what I helped create with my children and continued therapy until I had the strength and courage to start helping them. My children could only be who they were by the example that I set for them, and I know I did the best I could. For most of my life, I had been giving so much to others that I forgot about myself.

I was very good at supporting others in the business realm. I elevated people by giving them many compliments, and the more I elevated others, the more I undervalued and neglected to appreciate all that I brought to the table. I never did it intentionally. I did it because I wanted to show people love. Many years later, I would learn that the people in my life really wanted to know me. They wanted to spend time with me.

I only let people in so close until it felt uncomfortable for me. Once it became uncomfortable, I would shut down, and sadly, my children were in that context. I became a master at knowing how to do this even when I was with people without them even knowing it. It was a perfect fit for me to give mostly to clients and friends because I didn't have to live with them; I could give of myself for short periods, like appointments, phone calls, and emails. I kept everyone at an arm's distance; I only had to see and be with them every few weeks or most every couple of months. The conversations were always about their lives or what I could provide them in areas where they sought professional support. It was easier for me to see them than it was for me to take the time to see myself.

That summer of 2013, I recognized that I had taught my children how to have surface relationships without even realizing it. It was the only thing I knew, the only thing that was familiar to me, until I began the journey of unlearning what I had learned.

After realizing what I created and taking responsibility, changing it was simply a matter of putting in the time.

Nearly a year later, on Easter of 2014, my children had been away on their personal development journeys. Things were more stabilized to the extent that I felt like I could now just BE. This consisted of me resting and a lot of self care. I wanted to sit and reflect on all of the transformation that had occurred with me and my children over the past few months. I wanted my time and that is just what I gave me and I felt at peace with it.

First, I began to go through all of the pictures I had taken over the years and let go of the ones that no longer served me. This was a piece that I hadn't done with all of the Feng Shui I had done over the years. I never thought about it; I believe it came to me when I was ready to face it. Decluttering pictures and family memorabilia should be one of the last things to declutter because they are very personal. It makes sense why I waited subconsciously until the end to complete this portion of decluttering.

On Easter, I changed all of the family pictures I had in their frames to happy times, no matter what age I, my children, or other family or friends were in them. I got rid of some of the pictures from times that weren't so good and placed the many pictures I could not frame in a big vase shaped like a wine barrel with artificial grape vines in it. I had hundreds of photos that it would have been crazy to frame all of them. Instead, I wanted to place all the extra pictures in a beautiful and symbolic area.

This Easter day was different. I felt the urge to create a vision board to create everything I wanted. In the center of the vision board, I put the words: Healthy. Happy. Family. That's what I was determined to create.

My children's journey in transformational programs lasted over four years, and to this day, we still maintain them. It was a very difficult road to take. I used to wonder, "Why was I not able to help them?"

I beat myself up emotionally for years. It took me many years of healing workshops, training, books, and coaching to forgive myself and understand I did the best I knew how.

I loved my children through it all. I understand now that I had to learn how to love and accept myself before I could be someone to my children.

We had to work individually on being healthy in mind, body, and spirit before we could work on our family together. I learned that the best support and example for me was to live a passionate life. This meant I had to first find my passion and purpose, and so the journey of finding this began.

I learned I could only be with others how I am with myself, and now we all were in a time and space where we created just that. Once I forgave myself, I had the love for myself I always longed for from someone else. I was ready to let others in. I was ready to begin transforming my relationship with my children, friends and family.

After completing my vision board, I decided to go through all of my childhood papers that my mom recently gave me during the past Christmas. It was very eye-opening to go through these items. Some of the artwork I created as a child was depressing. As I looked at each piece I created as a child, I wondered what must have been going through my mind and how I was emotionally at this time. I was happy with how my life had changed over the years. Now, instead of sad, lonely paintings and pictures being in my home, everything had turned to brightness and beauty, the paintings, the pictures, the furniture, everything. I felt and saw beauty in everything.

When my son came to visit in 2015, I bought a movie theatre-style popcorn maker. It was everything I had always wanted. It was almost taller than me, and I stand about 5"4.

It had wheels and the whole bit. I bought this because it reminded me of my son. He loved popcorn so much while he was growing up. He thought it was a food group! The evening after I bought it, I was down in the basement in our theatre room working on putting it together. At that time, I was in a space where I wanted to do everything myself. I was avoiding my emotions and feelings of fear, anger, sadness, regret, and shame while he was visiting me, and this was an excellent way for me to stay busy. Putting this together helped me to avoid facing my feelings. Only there was one problem: I needed help putting it together, and I didn't know how, nor did I want to ask for the help I needed.

I was swearing left and right and hurt myself many times accidentally before my son came down to the basement to ask, "Do you need help, mom?"

I felt tears running down my face because he knew I needed him without me asking. This moment symbolized so much more to me than putting a popcorn machine together.

My son helped me learn how to receive help from a man again. In that very moment, I shifted to being vulnerable and open.

I let go and said yes, as tears were rolling softly down my face. He put that thing together so quickly and perfectly that I swear he had grown up right in front of my eyes. He was so patient and mechanical, and that moment helped me see just how much he had grown, and I could not have been a more proud mother. It was such a beautiful moment when I let all of my walls down.

I heard the message and the deliverer of the message, my son, loud and clear, and let go. I surrendered to another human being, a man, for the first time in I don't know how many years.

QUESTIONS AND ANSWERS

1. How is your relationship with your parents?

_____

_____

_____

2. Are you close with your children or siblings?

_____

_____

_____

3. What relationship in your life needs a little TLC?

_____

_____

_____

4. Who in your life do you feel you're ready to have a deeper connection with?

_____

_____

_____

Journal

CHAPTER 5

OPEN YOUR HEART

In September 2015, about a month after completing my shaman training, I found myself craving a different kind of growth. Shamanism had been a deep dive into healing—first myself, then guiding others through their own transformation. But now, my soul longed for something lighter, something that would soften me.

A friend recommended Keys to the Kingdom by Alison Armstrong. From the very first page, I was captivated. The story was told like a fairy tale, but the teachings were profound—centered on understanding men and the developmental stages they go through in life. I devoured it and, within a month, read every book Alison had written.

Her words awakened a part of me I hadn't realized had gone dormant. Somewhere along the way, I had become deeply masculine—always doing, achieving, providing. I had supported not just myself and my children, but also the men in my life. I was the giver, the rock, the provider. But I had forgotten how to receive.

And the truth was, I was exhausted.

My giving had become extreme. I showered people with things, trying to show love the only way I knew how. But I remember a friend once saying, "Stacie, stop giving me things. I just want time with you." I was stunned. It made me question everything.

What did I have to offer without the gifts?

Would I be enough just as I am?

I began to see how I had pushed people away by overgiving. I didn't know how to give of myself—my presence, my vulnerability, my heart. That realization was a turning point. I was ready to unlearn these patterns and open to a new kind of love.

I wanted a partner who would grow with me spiritually, emotionally, and intimately—a man who would support my dreams, see my worth, protect and adore me—as I would for him. But I didn't yet know how to receive that kind of love. I had to start within.

Months earlier, my relationship with Xavier had ended. For the first time, I wasn't the one walking away—he broke up with me. And it shattered me. I had never felt heartbreak like that. I couldn't sleep. I barely ate. I cried so much I thought the tears would never stop.

Xavier and I had a deep connection. We laughed, played cards, and cooked together. He wrote me poems, bought me sweet gifts, and made me feel cherished. He loved not only me but also my children. He showed up for me during the hardest seasons—when I was navigating my children's crises, managing the breakdown of my family, and holding my business together. Xavier believed in me when I couldn't believe in myself. His love felt like a first—unconditional and real.

But our relationship was also hidden. It was a secret from most of the people in our lives. And deep down, that didn't sit right with me. It mirrored my inner limitations—what I could receive at the time. Looking back, I can see that neither of us was fully available for the kind of partnership I craved.

After we broke up, I needed answers. Why did I keep attracting men who were emotionally unavailable or couldn't commit? Why did I end up in secret relationships or long-distance ones? What was the common thread?

Surprisingly, the answer came from one of my shaman teachers. I told him how exhausted I was from attracting the same kind of man, and he gently asked, "How are you not emotionally available to yourself?"

His words hit me like lightning. They unraveled something in me. I began to see myself more clearly—not as a victim of poor circumstances, but as the one common denominator in every relationship I'd ever had.

That's when I returned to Alison Armstrong's work, with a deeper hunger this time. I signed up for her course Understanding Men in October 2015. The class changed everything. I learned about the masculine and feminine energies within all of us. I learned how to communicate, listen, and honor the truth in myself and others. And more than anything, I learned that healing the masculine in me meant rediscovering the sacredness of my feminine essence.

I became obsessed with learning more. By the end of the course, I signed up for everything she offered. I needed to understand why I operated the way I did in relationships—why love had felt like a battlefield, even when everything else in my life looked so successful on the outside.

At that point, I had built a thriving business. I was respected in my industry, known for cultivating strong partnerships, and I had poured my heart into my work. But behind the scenes, my life felt hollow. I didn't have the kind of relationships I deeply longed for.

The business I had built with my father—my "first baby"—was no longer fulfilling. We had sold the company, and he retired the next day. I hadn't expected him to leave so suddenly. I grieved the loss of our shared mission and my father's daily presence in my life. At the same time, my children were struggling, my relationship had ended, and everything felt like it was unraveling.

I was drowning silently while holding it all together for everyone around me.

It became clear that I couldn't keep doing things the way I always had. My contract with the company was ending, and I had to decide whether to stay or leave. I longed to contribute in a new way, to bring heart and healing into the business culture. But when I proposed this to my boss, the answer was no.

That "no" cracked something open in me. I knew I had to walk away—not just from the company but from an entire identity I had built over two decades. With that, I submitted my resignation in December 2015.

It was terrifying. But it was also a homecoming.

I stayed on through March 2016 as a part-time consultant, but my heart was already shifting toward something new. That spring, I enrolled in Alison Armstrong's yearlong Professional Mastery training. I wanted to teach what had changed my life. Of course, I picked the topic that set the tone for all her teachings—a classic Stacie move: putting myself all in.

The program challenged me. There were interviews, presentations, public speaking, and personal breakthroughs. And just as I began to stretch into this new version of myself, I felt a pull—toward Italy.

Italy had been on my vision board for years. I always pictured going with the love of my life. But instead, I went alone. I decided to finish my next training presentation early and planned a solo trip to Italy, followed by a backpacking adventure through Ireland.

I hired a travel agent and filled my itinerary with art, wine, castles, and everything that delighted my senses. It was the first time I had planned something purely for me. I felt like a queen, dreaming and designing an experience for the woman I was becoming.

Italy cracked my heart wide open.

The beauty there was intoxicating. The vineyards, the cathedrals, the language, and the food all awakened a tenderness in me I had forgotten was even there. I fell in love... not with someone else but with myself.

I realized that the great love I had been searching for had to begin inside of me. I learned to receive beauty, to slow down, and to feel again. With every bite of fresh pasta and every walk through ancient streets, I remembered who I was beneath the armor I had worn for so long.

Italy became the place where my heart truly opened. Not for someone else to fill—but for me to finally come home to myself.

QUESTIONS & ANSWERS

1. What area of your life do you feel stuck in?

_____

_____

_____

2. Where are you resisting change?

_____

_____

_____

3. Where do you place your identity?

_____

_____

_____

4. What are you scared to let go of?

_____

_____

_____

5. What city or country would you go to alone if you could, and why?

_____

_____

_____

Journal

CHAPTER 6

HEALING CODEPENDENCY

COMING BACK FROM ITALY IN 2016, SOMETHING INSIDE ME HAD shifted. I returned with a renewed lease on life—a vibrant clarity pulsing through me, as though my soul had inhaled the air of freedom. I felt open and in love with my life—with myself. It was as if the beauty of the landscapes I had walked through had etched itself into my being, reminding me what it felt like to be truly alive.

When I got home, I only had a week before heading to a facilitator training in Denver with Alison Armstrong. Before Italy, I had already immersed myself in all of Alison's workshops—her teachings had helped me understand myself and the men in my life in ways I'd never thought possible. I learned how to communicate more effectively, how I had been communicating before, and how I could evolve. Most importantly, I discovered what I needed to feel whole—not just in a relationship, but within myself.

One of Alison's greatest gifts to me was illuminating the

distinction between a relationship and a partnership. That difference cracked something wide open in me. I realized what I had been seeking wasn't a relationship in the traditional sense—I longed for a sacred partnership. A soul-deep connection where two whole beings walk alongside one another, rooted in mutual support, reverence, and truth.

So I had continued her facilitator training, excited and passionate—but quickly, I realized it felt like too much. Italy and Ireland busted me open in a way that revealed how much healing I still needed. During the training in Denver, it became clear: I wasn't ready to lead others through this work. I needed to be with myself first. I needed to heal more deeply.

It was a hard decision to walk away. I've always been someone who finishes what she starts. But something deeper was speaking to me. And for the first time in a long time, I listened.

Afterward, I went to stay with my brother, sister-in-law, and their two little ones in Denver. The days were filled with walks, hikes, games, and conversations that filled my soul. There, nestled in the safety of family, something unexpected began: my journey into mixed media art.

My sister-in-law introduced me to painting with markers, stencils, stamps, paper, and texture. We began by creating angels. It was incredibly therapeutic. I would stay up into the early morning hours, covered in paint and surrounded by the quiet hum of creativity. It was like my soul had finally found a new language.

When I returned to Arizona, I bought all my own art supplies and began creating again—especially angels. At one point, I felt such a deep yearning to call in my future partner that I attempted to paint a man and a woman together. It was so hard for me to create the masculine figure. I stayed up all night, unwilling to stop until I brought them together on that canvas. It was more than art—it was a declaration, a prayer, a manifestation.

That marked a turning point. I paused taking classes and workshops and just started living. I wanted to call in my partner, so I began dating again. I took a course with a woman named Wendy who had gone on 101 first dates. Her course was about getting clear on what you wanted before the first date. It was so empowering.

I started dating off and on, learning more and more with each encounter. At the end of 2017, I met a man named Paul. It felt like we saw each other—soul to soul. For the first time, I shared pieces of my art, even though I still didn't feel entirely safe opening up about the deepest parts of my spirituality.

We continued dating into 2018, and near the end of our relationship, he introduced me to PSI Seminars, a transformational personal development organization. Their experiential learning cracked my heart wide open. I went through all their programs, which included week-long intensives on a ranch in California, team dynamics, and leadership of self and others. It was deep, soul-stretching work. Every exercise reflected how I was showing up in my life. I couldn't hide. I couldn't pretend. I could only meet myself.

The seminars helped me see where I quit—not always in action, but internally, emotionally. And because I've always been so committed to finishing what I start, I stayed. I kept volunteering as a coach to support others on their journey with the program and their life. I coached a 90-day leadership game called PLD—Pacesetter Leadership Dynamics—at least five times in three years. I watched people chase goals they never thought they could reach, and in the process, I healed parts of myself I didn't even know were fractured.

Though my romantic journey with Paul ended pretty quickly, I will always be grateful that he was the bridge to that work. More importantly, I gained hundreds of beautiful connections and a deeper, unshakeable connection with myself.

During that time, I kept dating here and there, still on the apps, trusting and searching despite not being my favorite way to connect with people; I much preferred the natural way. In 2019, I met a man on a first date—my now-husband, my eternal love. But I wasn't ready. He asked me out again, and I said no. We didn't exchange numbers. No closure. Just timing. The wrong time. Though I will always be grateful for dating apps because they brought me something better than I had always wanted, though I just didn't know it... YET...

So I kept going—dating, volunteering with PSI, growing. It was exhausting at times. Dating apps often felt draining, like they were siphoning my energy. I'd go on for a few weeks, then shut everything down for several weeks or even months. But deep down, I knew I had to be open to receiving love if I wanted love. I gave myself permission to be set up on blind dates, to meet people in person, to allow love to arrive however it was destined to.

Eventually, I learned a powerful truth: I was attracting who I was, not what I wanted. If I wanted to call in something different, I had to become the version of myself who truly believed she was worthy of that kind of love. And that required me to visit the places inside where love didn't live yet—where pain still echoed, where I still withheld compassion, acceptance, and love from myself.

In conversation with a girlfriend, I shared my realization about *why* my love life wasn't what I wanted. I was settling for breadcrumbs at best. She didn't waste any time telling me about a course she was certified in called *Calling in the One*. The work was based on a book with the same title.

I enthusiastically said YES before I knew what I was agreeing to. The course was supposed to take seven weeks, but it took me four months.

There were several deep, hidden wounds I couldn't see before, where I still sought validation outside of myself. I wasn't speaking compassionately to myself. I wasn't loving myself the way I thought. And I was still attracting emotionally unavailable men. Ultimately, I was always attracting men who would leave. And that fit because I bonded myself to my true self by choosing not to be who I was; instead, I would, as Alison taught me, "turn myself into a pretzel" out of my fear of them not liking me for who I am. My worthiness program was always in fight-or-flight. I just didn't know it until the beginning of 2020.

As the world spun out in panic for months that year, I dug in deep and went within. I got uncomfortable, and I yanked up deep roots that needed to be healed. Finally.

I remember that time of my life like it was yesterday.

One day, a dear friend sat with me, sensing the ache in my chest before I even spoke it out loud. She saw the pain I was carrying, the longing, the quiet knowing that I was settling for breadcrumbs. I didn't know how to name it then, but I knew it wasn't love—not the kind I dreamed of, not the kind I deserved.

And yet, I didn't know how to change it.

I didn't know how to stop contorting myself just to be chosen.

My friend was a relationship coach and when she offered to coach me, I said yes. Something in me was ready—even if I didn't yet know what that meant.

Over the next four months, everything shifted. Slowly, painfully, beautifully. I began to see what I hadn't been able to face before: I was twisting myself into knots, into something I was not—just to avoid the fear of being left again.

Like Allison Armstrong says, I was turning myself into a pretzel.

Out of fear. Out of scarcity. Out of this silent desperation to finally find "my person." I had done so much work over the years—so

103

much inner healing, reflection, spiritual growth—and yet, I was willing to settle.

I had a habit of settling for someone I knew wasn't right.

Someone who didn't truly see me.

Because in truth, I still wasn't fully seeing myself.

I wanted so badly to be ready for love, but in that longing, I bypassed the sacred truth that readiness doesn't come from forcing. Readiness is born from knowing, from honoring, from *being*. And I wasn't there yet.

Reading *Calling in the One* while working with my relationship coach cracked something open in me.

I realized I had no idea how deep I still needed to go.

I would have to meet myself at a level I hadn't yet touched to attract the kind of love I truly desired. I would have to be willing to hold compassion for the parts of me I had judged. I would have to stop pretending to be "fine," to stop hiding who I was beneath layers of spiritual armor.

I couldn't expect someone else to love the real me if I hid her.

I started asking myself hard questions:

Who am I, really?

What do I actually love?

Why am I afraid to share my spirituality—the most genuine part of me?

I stared at the paper, where I had just asked myself questions and couldn't get a single word down in answer form. My mind was blank. And that surprised me.

I asked myself another question: Why can't I find my answers?

The truth was, I was hiding from others because I was still hiding from myself. I *knew* who I was on some level. I just wasn't living it outside of my own private sacred space.

And in that hiding, I had created a fantasy version of love—a story that could never fully manifest because I wasn't entirely in it. I wasn't entirely me.

Externally, I was still very superficial in many of my relationships. But I was no longer a woman interested in holding surface-level connections or relationships. The more honest I got with myself, the more I realized I wanted to share the depth of all my pieces, beliefs, practices, and hobbies. And that meant opening up and sharing more. After all, I was a multi-layered woman with plenty to contribute to the world.

I love deep conversation and intimate connection.

I love art.

I love Feng Shui.

I love channeling.

I love meditation and the beauty of stillness.

I love presence.

I love spiritual and personal development.

And how could I ever attract a partner who truly sees and treasures those parts of me—if I wasn't honoring them in myself?

So, with every chapter of that book, every bonus practice, and every coaching call, I began to uncover pieces of myself I'd buried beneath layers of fear and self-protection.

And slowly, gently, I fell in love—with *me.*

Not in a surface way.

But in a soul way.

On a cellular level, I met myself.

And I started to trust her.

As much as I knew how to at the time... I loved her.

And that love would become the foundation for everything that came next.

At the end of 2020, in the wake of a year that changed the world, I started dating again. I met someone named Phillip. He checked a lot of the boxes. He was funny, spiritual, kind, retired, and had the freedom to travel to me since he didn't live in my state. I wasn't physically attracted to him, but I stayed curious because he checked so many boxes. I gave it time. I listened to my heart.

And then... in December of 2020, he surprised me by flying in for New Year's Eve. That night was beautiful. We laughed, shared dreams, clinked glasses. It felt like possibility. Like maybe, after all this time, the door to my heart was ready to open again.

He flew home the next day, with plans to return just a few days later so we could fly together to one of his homes in Colorado.

But life, as it often does, had other plans.

QUESTIONS & ANSWERS

1. What area of your life do you seek outside validation for?

_____

_____

_____

2. Think back to the last three triggers you experienced. Who/ What triggers you and why?

_____

_____

_____

3. What statement(s) below get a visceral response from you and why?
   a. I am unworthy.
   b. I am unlovable.
   c. I am not enough.

_____

_____

_____

4. What needs to change internally for you to let go of triggers and begin loving yourself at a deeper level?

_____

_____

_____

Journal

_____

_____

_____

_____

_____

_____

_____

_____

_____

_____

_____

_____

_____

CHAPTER 7

THE BROKEN ROAD

Dᴜʀɪɴɢ ᴛʜɪs ᴛɪᴍᴇ ᴏꜰ ᴍʏ ʟɪꜰᴇ, I sᴘᴇɴᴛ ᴍᴜᴄʜ ᴛɪᴍᴇ ᴠᴏʟᴜɴ-teering for others' personal development and growth. I loved watching people grow, heal, and evolve their consciousness. When I would volunteer, I took on the position of coaching others through their inner healing journey.

Life can't be all inner healing work, though. Sometimes, we need to blow off steam. So, a group of my friends I met through the personal development workshops I attended or volunteered for and I decided to take an off-road vehicle out into the desert one morning for some fun.

Word got out that a few of us were going to play in the desert, and others wanted to join. Before I knew it, we had a group of 10 people. We took turns riding and driving in the off-road vehicle. It was so fun, and the day was beautiful.

The vehicle had two driving modes —regular and super mode. I drove on the desert terrain and little hills in normal mode, feeling free and alive. I felt like I could take on the world and that all this work I'd been doing over the years had finally paid off. While driving around, I thought of the man I met from Texas. I was excited to see him again. Things felt like they were falling into place.

I remember laughing and squealing as sand kicked up behind the wheels. I drove back to where my friends were standing, expecting someone else to want to get behind the wheel. But instead, I was invited to take it back out again. My friend climbed into the passenger seat and dared me to put the car in Super Mode.

"You're on," I laughed.

Nothing could get me down that day. I was on a high.

We took off in Super Mode. It wasn't just the vehicle in Super Mode; it was me and my high, too. I loved it.

I couldn't stop laughing. Life was perfect. All that existed was the roar of the engine and the thrill of adventure.

There's a moment, a split second, where life as you know it changes. A before and after. A line drawn so sharply that you can never cross back over it.

For me, that moment came in not long after my Super mode high was introduced to a sickening force of impact.

THE MOMENT OF IMPACT

I saw the tree before me, but couldn't stop the off-roading vehicle from hitting it. It happened so fast—my hands gripping the wheel, my heart pounding, my breath catching in my throat. My friend and I were wearing helmets, body gear, all the protective equipment, and none of it could stop what was coming.

And then—impact.

A violent, gut-wrenching jolt as we slammed into the tree. I didn't realize that beneath the tree, hidden from view, was a ditch. The off-road vehicle plunged forward. I had no control over it. Fear overtook me. It was bigger than the pain. Bigger than anything else. In that moment, I couldn't stop what was happening. It was as if the universe had grabbed me from my Super mode high and slammed me against reality. I can still feel it now, just talking about it.

My first thought wasn't about myself; it was about my friend. I could barely breathe, but I managed to ask my friend if he was doing okay. I didn't wait for him to answer before I apologized over and over again.

I wanted to rip off my helmet and tear away the body gear constricting my ribs, though my body wasn't responding the way I wanted it to. I was trapped in pain, in shock, in a moment that didn't feel real.

My friend didn't seem to be as hurt as I was. I could feel the impact of the crash throughout my whole body. But mostly my back. I knew I had to get to a hospital. That was the only thing that mattered in that moment.

Somehow—though I don't even remember how—we returned to where our group was waiting. My body was shaking, freezing. My friend, ironically the one who was with me in the accident, rummaged through his vehicle, looking for anything to keep me warm. Of all things, he found a furry animal costume. It brought a little laughter to a serious situation, and for the moment, my shock and pain were dissipated. I wrapped myself in it, not caring how ridiculous it looked.

THE HOSPITAL ALONE IN THE UNKNOWN

My friends drove me to the hospital. The ride was a blur, pain and fear mixing into something I couldn't separate. When we arrived, reality hit me in a whole new way. My friends pulled to the emergency room entrance, and someone jumped out to get a staff member. It wasn't long before the doors opened and I was helped into a wheelchair.

It was the middle of COVID. No individuals were permitted to accompany me inside. I said good-bye to my friends and had to be wheeled into that hospital alone, terrified, in pain, and still in shock.

Everything happened at lightning speed once I got admitted. I was placed in a room, hooked up to a pain drip, dressed in a gown, and left alone for some time.

I kept wondering, *Am I paralyzed?* That thought looped in my mind. It didn't make sense, but fear isn't logical. I was in pain, but I didn't know how bad it was.

Would I need surgery?

How long will I be here?

What would happen next?

There was nothing I could do but surrender. I had no control. None. This was bigger than me. And in that moment, all I could do was turn inward—to the only thing that had ever truly held me in the darkest moments of my life: God.

Over the next week, I had test after test. It felt like it took forever to get answers to what happened to my body. I was given rules. I couldn't get up to use the restroom by myself. I couldn't walk around. I couldn't go anywhere without assistance.

Eventually, I was told that I had broken my back. It didn't require surgery, but escaped that route by a fine line.

The pain was physical, yes—but also emotional, and spiritual. It was devastating. And to make it even harder, Phillip—who had just been planning a getaway with me—was suddenly distant. He stayed in touch while I was in the hospital, but he never came. I know it was during COVID, and hospitals weren't allowing visitors, but even after I was discharged, he simply... disappeared.

So, there I was: not only healing from the trauma of a broken spine, but also tending to the deep wound of a heart that had just dared to hope again.

It was like a double heartbreak. Even triple. I had spent the better part of three years doing the deep inner work after Paul, preparing my heart, opening my spirit, and building the courage to believe in love again. To have that hope vanish felt crushing.

But sometimes, life cracks us open to reveal the places where love still needs to take root.

As I lay in bed—alone, aching, unable to move like I used to—I was forced to meet the parts of myself I had been avoiding. The places where I still longed to be chosen, the corners of my heart where I still expected someone else to bring me home to myself.

And that's when it began. The real healing. Not just of my spine, but of my soul.

This time, I realized the partnership I had longed for had to begin with me.

Me and God.

The deepest love story of all.

RECOVERY A LONELY ROAD THAT LED ME TO MYSELF

After the accident, everything changed. The pain, both physical and emotional, became my constant companion. But deep down, somewhere beneath the shock and trauma, a whisper rose from within me. It said, "You can heal. And you can do it your way."

So I vowed to myself that I would walk this path naturally. I was determined not to rely on surgery or prescription medications. And by what I can only describe as divine grace, I didn't have to. I was spared the knife. That, in itself, felt like a miracle. When I found out I didn't need surgery, relief flooded me. But that relief was short-lived. I wasn't strong enough to go home, so it was recommended that my next step was inpatient rehabilitation.

I was transferred to a rehabilitation hospital in a medical van to begin the long journey of learning how to move again, how to heal, and how to live in my new reality.

I made a choice. I would pour all of my intention and trust into the healing process and do it through love—love for my body, my emotions, my spirit.

The first significant step was getting off of pain medication. I knew I didn't want to stay on those prescriptions any longer than I had to. They dulled more than the pain—they dulled *me*. They made me foggy, heavy, disconnected. Within just a couple of weeks of being released from the hospital, I weaned myself off of them. It wasn't easy. My body still ached. My muscles screamed when I moved. But my soul was louder.

I signed up for physical therapy right away. Three times a week became my rhythm, a sacred appointment with my determination. I started reclaiming pieces of myself week by week, breath by breath. That six-month period of physical therapy wasn't just about my back—it was about me becoming whole again in mind, body, and spirit.

But I knew physical therapy alone wouldn't touch the layers of emotion buried in my body. That's when I turned to my naturopath and my chiropractor—a woman who was far more than that label could ever contain. She had been part of my wellness path for over a decade, and her work with methylation, craniosacral therapy, and deeply intuitive healing had always felt like medicine for my soul. She works with newborns, older adults, and everyone in between. I trusted her with everything.

Her hands, her wisdom, her presence—each visit was like a sanctuary. She didn't just adjust my spine. She helped release the grief and trauma that had taken root in my body, layer by layer. Each session reminded me that healing isn't linear. It's spiral-shaped. We revisit places, gently loosening the pain each time until it can finally leave.

Even in the hospital, I found unexpected sources of light. I remember being in the rehab facility—surrounded by machines and sterile air—and yet, I felt held by something greater. Every clinician I encountered felt like an angel placed there with perfect timing. I know that may sound strange, but it's true. Each person carried a unique gift.

One day, I wandered into the rehab gym and noticed the ceiling filled with hundreds of delicate paper snowflakes. They floated like prayers in midair. I asked if someone could show me how to make them, and the lead physical therapist—this radiant woman with the warmest eyes—took the time to sit with me in my room. She brought me supplies and showed me how to fold, cut, and create my own. That afternoon, we didn't talk about pain or muscles or exercises. We made snowflakes. And at that moment, I remembered that art heals, too.

Art became my medicine. Nurses began bringing me mandala coloring books, colored pencils, and crayons. I'd sit quietly and color for hours. Those little bursts of color reflected the beauty I was slowly reawakening within myself. With each stroke, I softened. I surrendered. I created a safe space inside of me through creativity itself.

When I got home, I kept following the thread of healing naturally. I shifted to supplements tailored to my body's unique needs. I focused on supporting my inner system—my hormones, my nervous system, my digestion. But there was still the matter of pain management. I didn't want to go back to anything that numbed me out or left me emotionally erratic.

So, I chose something that surprised even me: edibles. Gummies. Caramels. I had used them recreationally before, maybe once or twice a year. But now, they became sacred tools. Not for escape—but for soothing, relaxation, and quieting my system in the most gentle, loving way possible.

This wasn't about getting high. It was about grounding. About easing the tension in my body without flooding it with chemicals that would constipate me or swing my emotions like a pendulum. This was plant medicine, simple and straightforward.

Looking back now, I see what I couldn't see then: every choice I made was me choosing *me*.

Every snowflake I made.

Every supplement I took.

Every breath I exhaled in physical therapy.

Every time I said no to something that didn't feel aligned.

Every time I reached for art or herbs or color instead of prescriptions and pills.

I was building a new relationship with myself. A relationship rooted in trust, patience, love, and compassion. And this deep, unwavering love wasn't something I had ever fully known before. It wasn't romantic. It wasn't conditional. It was *sacred*.

A kind of love emerges when you nurture yourself through the darkest seasons of your life, when no one is watching. When you're not doing it to be seen, you do it because your soul is worth it. Because you know that you are a living, breathing miracle—and that miracles deserve reverence.

That's the love I found.

It's 2025 now, and I can finally see it clearly: that entire season of healing was never just about my back. It was about coming home to myself. It was about learning how to honor my body, voice, needs, and pace.

I don't regret the accident anymore. I wouldn't wish for it, no. But I *honor* it. Because it broke me open to a new way of living—one where I choose me. Again and again and again.

And in that choice, I found the greatest love I've ever known.

HEADING HOME

When I returned home weeks later, I returned to something even more complicated—complete aloneness.

No partner. No husband. No children to help me. It was just me. Me and my broken body and I. Me and the echoes of that crash replaying in my mind, and the fear of what my life would look like now.

I couldn't drive. I couldn't walk long distances. I couldn't ride a bike. Uber drivers became my lifeline for healing.

I had to rely on others to get me to doctor's appointments three or four days a week for physical therapy. Friends helped when they could, but I had to piece together my support system.

And then there were the in-between moments. The moments at home, alone, with nothing but my pain and my thoughts. Those were the hardest. I was met with an almost unbearable discomfort. Because healing wasn't just the physical pain from a broken back—but the emotional reckoning that came with it, it was about the emotions that surfaced when I had nowhere to run. It was about the fears, the grief, the frustration that I couldn't pretend away.

When I thought back to the man I was dating before the accident, I felt a new level of heartache. The heartache wasn't just about him disappearing on me. It was about opening up, being vulnerable and curious about someone, and starting over again.—one more time.

It was in those moments that I turned deeper into meditation—not just as something to do but as something that could help heal me. Teach me how to sit in stillness, how to be present with my body, my pain, and my emotions without running from them.

In that choosing, I began to see just how often I had left myself behind—how little compassion I held for my own pain, how deeply I believed love had to come from someone else to be real. In those first weeks, I didn't even enjoy my own company. But something miraculous began to unfold over the next six months.

Healing didn't just happen in my body.

It happened in my soul.

It happened in the quiet, in the tears, and in the moments when people showed up—not just physically but spiritually—to hold me in my humanness.

One day, after an Uber ride home from physical therapy, my driver asked if she could pray for me. A stranger. And in that moment, I let her. I opened. I shared. I didn't hold back. And something inside me cracked open even more—not from pain this time, but from receiving love. Not romantic love. Not expected love. But sacred love. Soul love. The kind of love that reflects who you are beneath the wounds.

And little by little, the world mirrored this love back to me.

Friends came over and simply lay beside me, holding my hand as I cried. Neighbors helped me out of bed. People brought groceries, cooked meals, and showed up in ways I never would have allowed before. And as I let them in, I let myself in.

This time, I didn't pretend to be fine.

This time, I didn't armor up.

This time, I practiced the most radical thing I'd ever known—vulnerability.

And in that vulnerability, I touched a wellspring of worthiness I never knew lived inside me. I realized I was lovable not because I was strong, self-sufficient, or "fine." I was lovable simply because I *am*.

And maybe that was the real healing all along.

Not the mended spine.

But the mended soul.

The moment I stopped waiting for someone else to choose me, I finally chose *me*.

Through the pain. Through fear. Through happiness, sadness, joy, laughter, the sorrow—through it all. Because healing isn't just about recovery, it's about rebirth. And I had come to believe through this process that we are constantly being reborn through every experience.

LESSONS FROM THE FALL

Everything happens in perfect divine timing, even though it may not always look how I want it to. Sometimes, that timing brings us discomfort, pain, and uncertainty. But even in those moments, something sacred is unfolding within us.

Here's what I learned in that space of brokenness:

1. **Surrender Is Not Defeat**

   I spent so much of my life pushing, striving, and proving myself. But this accident showed me that surrendering to the present moment—no matter how painful—wasn't weakness. It was the only way through. When we stop resisting reality, we create space for healing.

2. **Stillness Is Its Own Form of Movement**

   I thought healing meant getting back to where I was before. I was wrong. Healing was taking me somewhere new. In the stillness, I learned to listen—to my body, spirit, and the whispers of something greater guiding me toward a deeper understanding of myself.

3. **Pain Can Be a Teacher, If We Let It**

   Pain is loud and demands attention. But instead of running from it, I learned to ask, *"What is this here to show me?"* Pain carries messages about where we need care, where we need to release, and where we need to grow.

4. **We Are Stronger Than We Think, but We Are Not Meant to Do It Alone**

   I prided myself on being independent and on carrying my own weight. But when I couldn't even sit up without help, I had to learn to receive on a level I had never experienced before. And in that receiving, I found the deepest form of love.

THE GIFT OF MAX A NEW BEGINNING

And then, months after my healing journey, a beautiful gift arrived in my life—my puppy, Max.

From the moment he came home with me, I was no longer alone. His love, his energy, his presence filled the spaces that once felt empty. He became my companion, source of joy, and reminder that love shows up in the most unexpected ways. And I realized—through all of this and the pain and transformation—life was still giving me gifts.

Because healing isn't just about what we recover from, it's about what we open ourselves to.

But Max wasn't just a gift. He was a divine gift, a messenger, preparing me for what would come.

Within that same year, just a few months after my recovery, my life would change in ways I never dreamt possible. 2021 wasn't just the year I broke my back. It was the year I broke my heart *wide open*—to love, purpose, and my soul's destiny.

It was the year I fully stepped onto my *Heartist's Journey*—a deeper journey into myself.

My healing didn't stop with me.

I was so profoundly grateful for the care and support I received during my recovery that I knew I had to give back. The doctors, nurses, physical therapists, and the entire hospital group that had helped me regain my strength had given me a second chance at life, and I wanted to do something in return.

So, I started a fundraiser for the rehabilitation hospital that had been there for me when I needed them most. What started as a gesture of gratitude grew into something larger. With the support of friends, family, businesses, and a community that believed in my cause, I raised **$40,000 in just four months** to give back to the place that had given me so much.

It was one of the most humbling and fulfilling moments of my life—to know that my journey, pain, and healing could now help others on their own path to recovery.

I ended 2021 much differently than it began. I retired from the company I had built for 23 years. I closed a chapter that had defined so much of my life, trusting that something greater was waiting for me. And in choosing *me*—in choosing love for myself, my spirit, and my heart—I walked into the life I was always meant to live.

And then in the spring of 2022, a little over a year after my accident, love found me most divinely.

Three years after the first date, I met *him* for the second time.

My eternal divine partner. My best friend. My world.

The one who would show me what eternal love truly feels like, both within and with him, would walk this journey with me, not just as a companion, but as a soul intertwined with mine.

I could have never known, in those moments of pain, in the depths of loneliness and surrender, that life was preparing me for this. Everything was unfolding in divine timing, even when it didn't look how I wanted it to or how I thought it should. It was something better!

That's the thing about life: It always leads us home, home to the love that we are.

AN INVITATION TO YOU

Maybe you haven't broken your back. Maybe your breaking came in the form of loss, heartbreak, or an unexpected turn in your own journey. But I know this: we all have our falls.

What matters is what we do with them.

Because sometimes, the fall doesn't just break us—it breaks us open.

And what's waiting on the other side might be the most beautiful gift. Something better than we could ever imagine.

QUESTIONS & ANSWERS

1.   Now, take a deep breath and ask yourself: Where am I resisting?

_____

_____

_____

2. Take another few rounds of deep breathing and ask yourself: Where am I trying to force my way through something that might require surrender?

_____

_____

_____

3. Who can you turn to when you are at your most vulnerable? Consider the things you love and trust about your person are the things you love and trust about yourself.

_____

_____

_____

4. We all experience physical pain. Think back to a time you were hurting physically and ask yourself: What is this here to show me?

_____

_____

_____

Journal

CHAPTER 8

WHEN THE SOUL KNOWS

Mᴀ ʟɪꜰᴇ ꜱʜɪꜰᴛᴇᴅ ᴇxᴘᴏɴᴇɴᴛɪᴀʟʟʏ ᴀɴᴅ ᴜɴᴇxᴘᴇᴄᴛᴇᴅʟʏ. Iᴛ ᴡᴀꜱ as if the Universe whispered—softly yet with undeniable clarity—"Now."

I had just completed coaching my final round of PLD, a journey that had molded, stretched, and brought me back to myself. A chapter had closed, and with it came a sacred opening. I was re-entering the dating world—open-hearted, steady, and no longer searching to fill a void. I had returned home to me.

And then, as if perfectly timed by something greater, Phillip resurfaced. He came to see me near my birthday. It had been over a year, and I had done my soul work—I had healed, cried, and remembered who I was. I greeted him not with old patterns, but from a place of peace and presence. I forgave. I allowed what was to be, unattached to any outcome, simply. And as I continued to walk forward with trust, something more divinely aligned emerged.

Eric.

He messaged me out of the blue—yet not random at all. A simple birthday note from someone I'd only been on one date with three years prior. We'd never exchanged numbers. We weren't connected online. And yet, he found his way to me.

"I always thought you were really cool," he said. "I remembered it was your birthday. How are you?"

I stared at the message in disbelief. My heart pounded—not from fear, but from recognition. Stay open, my soul whispered. And I listened.

We went to lunch. Technically, it was our second first date. But this time, I truly saw him: his humility, the way he spoke of his son, his unwavering loyalty to friends, his kindness to the server, his humor, his warmth, his light. There was no mask, no façade. Just truth. Gentle. Present. Real.

What astonished me even more was who he was in that moment... never changed. The man I met that day continues to show up for me every single day—not in grand gestures or perfect lines, but in his presence, consistency, and deep, unwavering heart.

Life seemed to guide us forward with grace as we spent more time together. There were still other dates I had committed to, and Phillip eventually drifted out of my life again—this time without pain. It felt like a divine clearing, as if God was gently making room for what was always meant to be.

Eric and I laughed endlessly. There was this effortless joy from the beginning—like we had been playing together across lifetimes. We often joke that our second first date didn't even count. "You weren't even into me!" he teases. And I always smile, "It's not that I wasn't into you. I just wasn't ready for you until now."

One month later, he asked me to be his girlfriend. A simple moment that landed like a sacred vow. Two months later, we moved in together. But just before that transition, he got scared. The depth of our connection overwhelmed him. For a moment, he pulled back. And I—grounded, centered, clear—stood in the truth of our love. "There's no way we're breaking up," I said. "We're meant to be together."

He knew it too. Deep down, he always knew.

From then on, our lives became a shared journey of growth, joy, and spiritual expansion. Eric supported my creative expression, cheering me on as I taught Art From the Heart and led retreats. He even discovered his own artistry through it, surprising both of us with how deeply the creative current ran through him.

He joined me in my world of spiritual studies, attending classes at Delphi University, meditating beside me, and sitting in a circle. Watching him embrace his own path of inner discovery has been one of the most beautiful experiences of my life. It's not just that we love each other—it's that we see each other. We walk together not just as partners but as mirrors, as medicine, and as sacred companions.

As he supported my dreams, I supported his—his business, his music, his friendships, his fatherhood, his healing. I witnessed his light expanding, and it brought me to tears more times than I can count.

We belly laugh every day—like, lose-your-breath, cry-your-eyes-out laughter. Eric is hilarious. His wit is brilliant, and his timing impeccable. The joy he brings to my life is uncontainable. We travel the world, yet some of our most cherished memories are the quiet nights at home—grilling in the backyard, solving puzzles, playing backgammon, sharing stories, and simply being together in the warmth of our love.

And then, just when I thought it couldn't get more magical...

We got married.

In 2025, on sacred sand in Mexico, we said our vows. We had just completed a profound Connecting with the Creator workshop, and the air around us shimmered with Spirit. The veil between worlds felt so thin that day. We could feel the presence of angels, ancestors, and God.

Everything about that moment—our bare feet in the sand, the ocean wind, the sound of our dear ones singing and blessing us—was divinely orchestrated. It wasn't just a wedding. It was a remembering. A homecoming. A soul ceremony across dimensions.

People still tell us they can feel our love when we walk into a room. That it moves them, awakens them. And that is our shared prayer: to be a living example of what love can look like when two souls surrender fully to their truth, their healing, and to one another.

This union isn't just romantic. It's devotional. We are partners in life, in spirit, in creation. We are here to walk one another home—and to help light the way for others as they walk toward their own sacred love.

So if you're reading this, wondering if that kind of love is real, or if it's possible for you...

Please believe me when I say: It is. It's not just possible, it's destined. Stay open.

It all begins with a whisper.
A decision to stay open.
To walk through the fire.
To come home to yourself.

And then one day, love walks in—
Not to save you, but to *meet you*.
To walk with you.
To remind you of everything you already are.

And so, this is how the story softens to a close—
not with a period, but with a pulse.
A promise.

A life once cracked open now blooms with grace.
The girl who once questioned her worth
became the woman who claimed her place
in the arms of love that never left—
only waited.

Waited for her to remember who she was.
Waited for him to arrive when the stars aligned.
Waited for the moment when two paths
would become one prayer, spoken in silence,
heard by the heavens.

We are not promised a perfect life.
But we are promised a path—
one that leads us home,
not to a place,
but to a person
who holds the mirror
and says, "There you are."

This love—
this sacred, soul-spun, holy kind of love—
was never meant to be ordinary.
It was meant to be a lighthouse.
A testament.
A remembering.

And now we walk, hand in hand,
into forever.

Not as the ending.
But as the beginning
of all that was always meant to be.

And so, this is how the story softens to a close—
not with a period, but with a pulse.
A promise.

A life once cracked open now blooms with grace.
The girl who once questioned her worth
became the woman who claimed her place
in the arms of love that never left—
only waited.

Waited for her to remember who she was.
Waited for him to arrive when the stars aligned.
Waited for the moment when two paths
would become one prayer, spoken in silence,
heard by the heavens.

We are not promised a perfect life.
But we are promised a path—
one that leads us home,
not to a place,
but to a person
who holds the mirror
and says, "There you are."

This love—
this sacred, soul-spun, holy kind of love—
was never meant to be ordinary.
It was meant to be a lighthouse.
A testament.
A remembering.

And now we walk, hand in hand,
into forever.

Not as the ending.
But as the beginning
of all that was always meant to be.

EXERCISES

In this section, you will create your next phase of your Heartist Journey through story. There are studies that show our heart emits an electrical field 60 times greater than our brains and an electromagnetic field 5,000 times stronger than our brains.

Imagine what we can create when we *feel* into what we desire instead of simply thinking about it, or writing down a list of attributes and qualities that we want in our dream life. Emotions and feelings have a stronger magnetic attraction than our thoughts. When you embody strong emotions associated with your desires, you are influencing the quantum field and you will become a magnet for your desires.

Below, instead of writing out what you want in a partner, write out what you look forward to experiencing with someone. Write it in the present tense. And afterward, read it out and allow yourself to hold the feeling that washes over you. Meditate in it.

Write Your Dream Life in Present Tense Below:

The next exercise is to visualize your dream life playing out in front of you like a movie. Our subconscious cannot determine if what you're imagining is real or not. And the longer you visualize something playing out in front of you, while you're holding the feeling associated with it, the more impactful this exercise will be for you.

_____

_____

_____

_____

_____

_____

_____

_____

_____

_____

_____

YOUR CELEBRATION LIST

Finally, we will celebrate your Dream Life as if it were already here. How are you celebrating your life together? Did you envision traveling with your partner? Do you have a new home and dinner parties? Did you celebrate your latest book with your partner? Share your wins and how you celebrate with your new partner in your Dream Life below.

To help you get started, here are some prompts:

What kinds of things are you experiencing?

How do you interact with others, and how do they interact with you?

What FEELINGS do you feel being in this DREAM LIFE?

Imagine there are NO LIMITS—What are your heart's DEEPEST Limitless Desires in your DREAM STORY? (If limiting beliefs arise, simply notice, release them, and keep tapping into what your heart wants)

Who must I BE in this DREAM LIFE?

Journal

Create Your Own Mandala

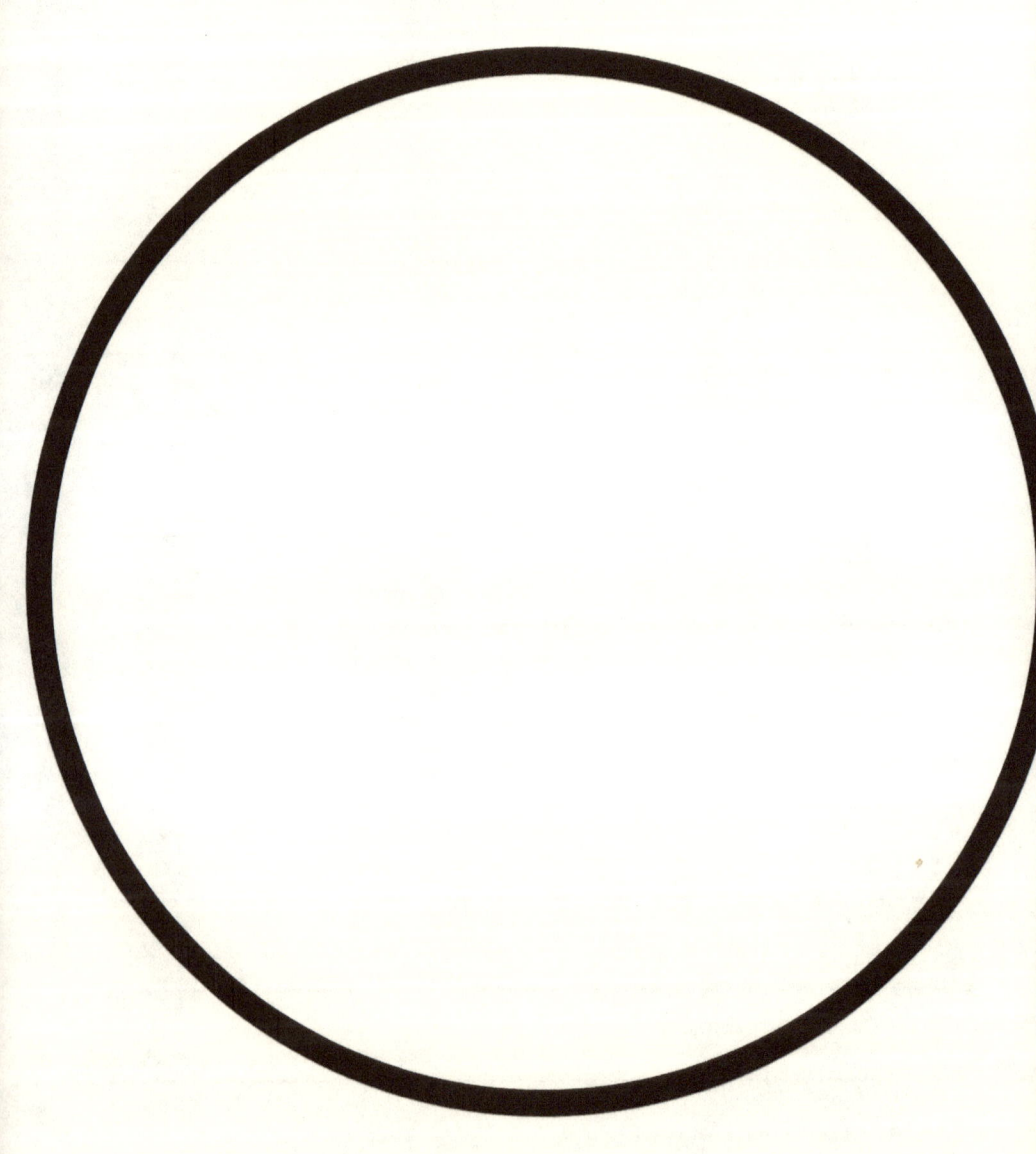

EPILOGUE

I ARRIVED AT DELPHI SPIRITUAL UNIVERSITY ON MARCH 4, 2025, to continue obtaining my Doctorate in Entura Art and receive healings.

While I was there, I was to receive a three-day-long deep therapy called Rohun.

The day that therapy was finished, Delphi hosted a healing session they hold every first Friday of the month—a day open to all, free of charge, where intentions are set and doors to the unseen are opened. When I arrived, I carried one clear intention in my heart: to heal my migraines for good. I thought I was simply asking for physical relief, but I had no idea the journey this request would take me on.

Twelve days passed, yet it felt like lifetimes had moved through me. I have walked through healing so profoundly that time has stretched, shifted, and dissolved. In the vast stillness of this place, I have met myself in ways I never had before.

What I thought was a physical ailment turned out to be a reflection of something much deeper—the ways I have suffered through my healing. Not just the pain, but the suffering within the pain. The relentless self-judgment, the anger at myself for not "getting there" fast enough, the control I gripped onto so tightly that I hadn't allowed my emotions to move freely through me. My migraines weren't just migraines. They embodied every unprocessed feeling, every moment I had turned against myself instead of toward myself. What I thought was carried in a migraine was carried throughout my body.

As I moved through Rohun, First Friday, and the first of my three classes, my body finally spoke in a way I could not ignore. The migraine arrived like a tidal wave days after the First Friday healing— pulsing, consuming, unrelenting.

I was quiet about my migraine as I did not want to give it energy or attention, so I curled up in my room away from everyone when we were not in class, the pain pressing against my skull, as if all the lifetimes I had carried were trying to break free at once.

A soft knock at my door.

"Is there anything I can do to help?"

The voice was gentle, filled with a kindness I didn't know how to receive at that moment. I opened my eyes to see a classmate standing there, her presence steady and unwavering.

I hesitated, my instinct telling me to bear this alone, but something softer within me whispered, Let go.

"Do you do bodywork?" I asked, my voice barely carrying through the pain.

She nodded and stepped inside.

I had never felt so vulnerable. The walls I had so carefully built— against pain, against love, against being fully seen—began to crack. She didn't just touch my body; she held space for something much more profound.

She guided me to ask my body, "What do you need?"

The question hovered in the air. I wanted to say relief, but I knew that wasn't the answer. I closed my eyes, feeling the raw edges of my resistance.

"Grace," I whispered. "I need grace."

She met my gaze, understanding without words.

And then the tears came.

Not just tears from the pain, but from the sheer weight of my resistance breaking open. I hadn't realized how much I had been withholding from myself—love, compassion, gentleness. I had been demanding healing instead of allowing it.

She encouraged me to ask for help, not just from her, but from something greater. So I did.

Through tears, through surrender, I turned inward. "Creator, help me find grace," I whispered. "Help me experience grace through my healing."

And something shifted.

The healing did not come in a single, dramatic moment. It came in waves over the next few days, in breath, in allowing.

In the days that followed, I went through more healings, each one revealing the same truth—I had been resisting a deeper layer of love. Every cell in my body had been clenched in control, afraid to receive what I needed most.

But as the days unfolded, I slowly began to release, little by little.

Control softened. Judgment loosened its grip. The deep resistance to grace—the belief that I had to suffer through healing and earn my own worthiness—began to dissolve.

I stood on my EDGE. And instead of pushing forward, I surrendered to it.

I found something I had never known on the other side of that edge.

A grace so deep, so all-encompassing, it filled every space I had once held with self-judgment.

A love that asked nothing of me, except to be received.

A forgiveness that wrapped around my past and whispered, You were never meant to carry this alone.

As I sit here now, I can barely put into words the depth of what I feel. Peace, acceptance, love—everything washing over me in ways I could have never imagined.

I came here asking for healing. What I found was grace.

ABOUT THE AUTHOR

Stacie Sholer has a heartfelt passion for helping individuals on their individual journeys of self-discovery. She is a spiritual mentor, reiki master, shaman, and has a doctorate in entura artist/ therapist, level three connecting with the creator practitioner and the creator of "The Heartist Journey" — a creative methodology that helps you get in touch with your heart through art and other various creative outlets.

Through all that she does, she seeks to show people how to cultivate more alignment, acceptance, love, and abundance in their lives.

Since retiring from her corporate career in 2021, she's devoted herself to helping others discover and live their purpose. With 28 years of experience studying EQ, field of human potential and spirituality, she integrates healing modalities and creative practices to guide her clients, whom she fondly refer to as heartists, toward inner love and harmony.

She believes in the power of creativity to foster a deep connection with the self, leading to greater self-acceptance and self-love. She also believes the love we each crave outside of the self starts from within. Her approach is rooted in nurturing, heart-centered principles to help guide each individual heartist on their own unique journey toward fulfillment through spiritual mentorship, private and group classes and workshops.

Her own spiritual journey began in 2001, where she began to obtain the goals she set for herself by discovering and changing something internally first. After recovering from a tragic back accident in 2021, she dove even further into self-discovery work and set out to create a way that gives others the tools to transform their own lives. Thus, "The Heartist Journey" was born.

The accident also inspired her to write her first book, "The Heartist Journey," and create Catching Snowflakes, a fundraiser supporting the Bob Bové Neuroscience Institute at HonorHealth.

She continues to invest in her spirituality, expanding the reach of all of classes, workshops and other services that she offers. She resides in Phoenix, Arizona, with her loving and supportive husband, Eric and their snuggly fur baby Max.